CUÉNTAME

CUÉNTAME

Narrative in the Ecclesial Present

by

NATALIA IMPERATORI-LEE

ORBIS BOOKS

Maryknoll, New York 10545

ORBIS BOOKS
Maryknoll, New York 10545

Fathers and Brothers
MARYKNOLL™
TOGETHER IN GOD'S MISSION OF MERCY

Founded in 1970, Orbis Books endeavors to publish works that enlighten the mind, nourish the spirit, and challenge the conscience. The publishing arm of the Maryknoll Fathers and Brothers, Orbis seeks to explore the global dimensions of the Christian faith and mission, to invite dialogue with diverse cultures and religious traditions, and to serve the cause of reconciliation and peace. The books published reflect the views of their authors and do not represent the official position of the Maryknoll Society. To learn more about Maryknoll and Orbis Books, please visit our website at www.maryknollsociety.org.

Library of Congress Cataloging-in-Publication Data

Names: Imperatori-Lee, Natalia M., author.
Title: Cuentame : narrative in the ecclesial present / by Natalia Imperatori-Lee.
Description: Maryknoll : Orbis Books, 2018. | Includes bibliographical references and index.
Identifiers: LCCN 2017045183 (print) | LCCN 2018005572 (ebook) | ISBN 9781608337330 (e-book) | ISBN 9781626982673 (pbk.)
Subjects: LCSH: Hispanic American theology. | Hispanic Americans—Religion.
Classification: LCC BT83.575 (ebook) | LCC BT83.575 .I47 2018 (print) | DDC 262/.0208968—dc23
LC record available at https://lccn.loc.gov/2017045183

For Michael, William, and Benjamin,
my favorite characters,
with gratitude for our story

Contents

Acknowledgments

A central thesis of U.S. Latinx theological anthropology is that human beings are inherently communal and social, that they are always already woven into preexistent, unchosen communities that constitute identity. The six-year journey to the completion of this book has reminded me time and again of the many ways in which community is necessary and inescapable. Our very existence is possible because of the myriad ways in which communities of care and concern surround and support us. As scholars, we depend on community for instruction and correction, and I have been blessed with talented, careful colleagues throughout my theological journey.

I owe deep gratitude to Mary Catherine Hilkert, J. Matthew Ashley, Timothy Matovina, and the rest of the faculty of theology at the University of Notre Dame for their mentorship and their continuing friendship. My colleagues at Manhattan College have been a constant source of encouragement through this process, especially Michele Saracino and Judith Plaskow, who heard my early ideas for this book and cheered on my efforts throughout the process of writing. My colleagues at the Dante Seminar at Manhattan College also received early versions of sections of this book and offered incisive questions and helpful comments. I was afforded time to research this project and do some writing through a sabbatical grant from Manhattan College, as well as through the help of the Faculty Development Program, which provided a yearly course release that freed up some time during the semester. My students at Manhattan College are my greatest teachers, and I am particularly grateful to all the students in my U.S. Latino/a Catholicism courses, who encourage me with their persistence, patience, and embrace of hybridity.

The Catholic Theological Society of America has become a sort of theological home for me, and I am grateful to have had the opportunity to present some of this work at two conventions and to have received excellent feedback from both the Practical Theology group and the panel on the sense of the faithful at the 2015 convention. Edward Hahnenberg of John Carroll University has been a faithful companion on this ecclesiological road with me since our graduate student days at the University of Notre Dame, and his enthusiasm for the project, coupled with his excellent feedback on specific chapters and wealth of knowledge about the sense of the faithful, has improved this text tremendously. I am deeply indebted to him.

I must acknowledge my gratitude as well to the members of the Academy of Catholic Hispanic Theologians in the United States (ACHTUS), who were the first audience for these ideas, and who believed in the project and improved it with their insight and *acompañamiento*. I am aware that much of what I have I owe to the pioneering work of those scholars, and my responsibility to open doors for future generations is not lost on me. María Teresa Dávila, Hosffman Ospino, María Pilar Aquino, Jorge Aquino, and many, many others whom I am fortunate to call companions on this journey of scholarship and friendship sustain me with their accompaniment in thought and prayer.

None of this work would have been possible had I not been blessed with a family that believed in my education and convinced me early on that I could succeed as a scholar. My parents and grandparents instilled in me a love of learning; my Abuelo Pepito took me to the library before I could read and taught me to love literature and poetry; and my maternal grandparents, Melva Luisa Cedeño and Antonio Rodriguez, educated me with their example of hard work and fierce love. My parents, Maria Victoria and Alberto Carlos Imperatori, prioritized their children's education above all else, and provided a home filled with love and laughter. I hope this book reflects some of the fruits of their labor as well.

My whole Miami community has offered generous emotional and material support for this project. I want to thank in a special way the members of the Agrupación Católica Universitaria, who were willing to be interviewed for this book: Emilio de Armas, Marty Perez, David Prada, and Guillermo Garcia-Tuñon S.J., as well as the many friends who served as intermediaries for me in setting up these interviews: Christina Gomez, Natalie Plasencia-Calvo, Isabel Ordaz, and Jeffrey Caballero. Many of these relationships were forged when we were all in high school, and I'm grateful to Our Lady of Lourdes Academy for prioritizing women's education and theology within that. In a very special way, I want to thank Elsie Miranda, now of Barry University, who was my first teacher of "real" theology at Lourdes, and from whom I continue to learn in friendship and joy.

Many communities of friends have supported me when I did not think this project would ever come to light. Brenna Moore and Maureen O'Connell buoy me with love and laughter, and without their encouragement and commiserating this book would not exist. To April Brown, Lara Dua-Swartz, and Jennifer Petras, who share a breakfast table with me every Friday, I owe my sanity and my strength.

The entire staff at Orbis Books has been fantastic, patient, and professional over the past four years. I want to thank my editor, James Keane, for his humor and intellect, and his holy patience as I struggled to bring this project to fruition. Robert Ellsberg, Maria Angelini, and the entire staff at Orbis believed in this project and worked hard to bring this book to light.

Lastly, I am indebted to my own little family for the many ways in which their love has enlightened me and invited me to explore new ideas in different ways. My boys, William and Benjamin, have taught me how to maximize my time and how to love beyond measure. I want to thank them specifically for their suggestions toward the end of this process, that I finish the book by writing supercalifragilisticexpialidocious repeatedly, or that I add a story about a tree. My spouse, Michael E. Lee, is heroic in his companionship and loyalty, in his commitment to our family, and in his organization and ability to keep us all well nourished physically and spiritually. There is no way to thank him for always thinking of others before himself, for being a true partner in my life, for believing in me and in my work in tangible ways, like giving me time and space to think in the midst of the bustling reality that is family life. Whatever success and happiness I enjoy is ours, and never mine alone.

Introduction

"Cuéntame"

> There is a certain embarrassment about being a story-teller in these times when stories are considered not quite as satisfying as statements and statements not quite as satisfying as statistics, but in the long run, a people is known, not by its statements or its statistics, but by the stories it tells.
>
> —Flannery O'Connor
> *Mystery and Manners*

The title of this book is essentially an invitation to tell a story. One of my earliest memories, in fact a regular facet of my growing up, was hearing my mother settle in to a phone call, often with her own mother or a close friend, and say in a very drawn out way, *"A ver, cueeeeentame."* Her intonation rang like the beginning of something, usually a long conversation in which the interlocutors would touch base, report on the latest news in their lives, analyze whatever familial conflict or joy was going on at present, and generally just share their lives. Her voice in those words was an invitation to sit down and chat, and for a curious child like me, to sit close by and listen. This is quite literally what the word *cuéntame* means; the first-person reflexive form of *contar*, which means "to count or tell." In English, the words "account" and "recount" carry some of this double meaning: to tell a story and also to do a proper accounting. I hope to intone this double definition throughout this work, which focuses on the power of stories to properly account for the experience of the people of God.

My mother had a habit of doodling words on random scraps of paper while talking on the phone, with the result that I could often reconstruct the latest family news or friendly gossip by picking up the notes she left behind, if I couldn't piece it together from her side of the conversation. I learned much from sitting nearby when she was on one of these phone calls—what family members were visiting soon, who if anyone was planning to leave Cuba and when and how, and how long they'd be staying at my house, what the latest illness/engagement/birth/death meant for everyone in my house, and much more. I also learned the complexity of my family history, and my family's stories: the building blocks of my identity.

This text tries to respond to an invitation to tell a story, namely, the story of the church. But this story cannot be told in a general or merely "objective, historical" sense. Rather, like all good stories, the story of the church told here will be very particular, rooted in the experience and lives of Latino/a Catholics in and near the United States. It will also be multifaceted and interdisciplinary, because a good story touches on and meshes with other narratives. A good ecclesial story should incorporate historical, literary, and social-scientific evidence in the hopes of elaborating a new way of understanding the reality of the church.

In the past, ecclesiological works have focused on dogmatic principles and their expression in the church.[1] Theological manuals treated the church as a *societas perfecta* (perfect society), where each rung of the church from the pope down through the hierarchy to the clergy fulfilled spe-

---

1. See Richard P. McBrien, *Catholicism* (New York: HarperCollins, 1994), or Richard P. McBrien, *The Church: The Evolution of Catholicism* (New York: HarperCollins, 2008), among others.

cific duties. The laity, at best, aided in the apostolate of the clergy, and at worst were colloquially there to "pay, pray, and obey." Treatises meant for seminary training centered on the marks of the church, or images taken from scripture and tradition, the doctrines of salvation, membership in the church, or the distinctiveness of Catholicism. Only afterward, or as a second moment, did ecclesiology consider how these concepts apply to the church, the people of God.

Attuned to the horizontalizing influence of the Second Vatican Council, particularly its emphasis on the baptismal dignity of all believers who share in Christ's roles of priest, prophet, and king, this foray into ecclesiology focuses instead on the praxis and experience of the Latino/a communities in the United States in an effort to move away from abstract, static, or idealized notions of church and toward a more robust vision of the pilgrim people of God hinted at in the documents of Vatican II. Rather than deduct ecclesiology from principles, the time has come to attempt an inductive approach, beginning with praxis.

The field of Latino/a theology has existed since the mid-1970s, contributing rich insights to theological anthropology, theological method, and Christology. Still, no comprehensive ecclesiological tract has emerged from the theologians who work in this field. Three Latino theologians have made significant contributions toward an ecclesiology from a Hispanic perspective, Gary Riebe-Estrella, Roberto Goizueta, and most influentially Orlando Espín, but none has written a complete ecclesiology or a substantial treatment of ecclesiological themes.[2] After his seminal publication on Hispanic

---

2. See Gary Riebe-Estrella, "Pueblo and Church," in *From the Heart of Our People: Latino/a Explorations in Catholic Systematic Theology,* ed. Miguel H. Díaz and Orlando O. Espín (Maryknoll, NY: Orbis Books, 1999), 172–88); Roberto S. Goizueta, *Caminemos con Jesús* (Maryknoll, NY: Orbis Books, 1995); and Orlando O. Espín, *The Faith of the People* (Maryknoll, NY: Orbis Books, 1997), as paradigmatic among these thinkers' works.

Catholic ecclesiology, "Pueblo and Church," Riebe-Estrella focused on pastoral theology as well as theological education. Goizueta has written extensively in various fields within systematic theology, most recently Christology, aesthetics, and justice, but often with an ecclesial inflection. The theologian who has examined ecclesiological themes most extensively has been Espín, with groundbreaking essays on tradition, the *sensus fidelium*, reception, and popular religious practices, as well as more recent work on anthropological and aesthetic topics in systematics.[3] Methodologically, Latina theologians such as María Pilar Aquino and Ada María Isasi-Díaz made significant contributions to Latinx theology, and though the work of both will figure here, neither would consider herself a specialist in ecclesiology.

A Latinx ecclesiology must be rooted in practice and experience, and therefore invite a reorientation of ecclesiological method more broadly, and take narrative seriously as a starting point in both these tasks. To say *cuéntame* is an invitation to dialogue, a demand to tell—to narrate—the reality of life in its messiness and complexity. In doing this, in narrating the circumstances of our lives, or our worries, or our joys, we build relationships and strengthen ties, and we take par-

---

3. It is difficult to overstate the importance of Espín's work to Latinx theology, specifically to the study of popular Catholicism and its centrality to the fields of theological anthropology, aesthetics, liturgy, and ecclesiology. From his seminal text on popular Catholicism, *The Faith of the People: Theological Reflections on Popular Catholicism* (Maryknoll, NY: Orbis Books, 1997), Espín has elevated the devotion and praxis of Latinx communities to a true *locus theologicus,* and elevated the interplay of religion and culture to a *sine qua non* in contemporary Catholic theology. His more recent work on tradition and culture, *Idol and Grace: On Traditioning and Subversive Hope* (Maryknoll, NY: Orbis Books, 2014), bridges his ecclesiological work on the laity and particularly the marginalized to an eschatological vision of hope as a virtue that is traditioned in contextual ways. Throughout this work, Espín is a crucial conversation partner and teacher, a pioneer in thinking ecclesiologically *latinamente.*

ticular stock of ourselves, creating and maintaining identity, memories, and hope.

But the verb *contar* has an additional meaning. Besides "to tell," *contar* signifies "to count," or "to include"—similar to its English cognate, where count can refer to numerical counting or to something like reliance: "count on me." Thus *cuéntame* can also be rendered as a demand: do not leave me out, be sure I am accounted for. This is critical for many contexts in which the participation of U.S. Hispanics is either underrepresented or altogether overlooked. This omission is the result not of a lack of theology or theological reflection—indeed the earliest Catholic theology done in America was done in Spanish, and Latinos and Latinas have long made significant contributions to the tradition—but rather the omission is a result of false or falsifying narratives that render a contingent of the population invisible. *Cuéntame* is as much imperative demand as it is alluring invitation to dialogue, and this demand is not merely that a story be told but that all voices be counted/accounted for in the telling.

In other words, it is not merely a matter of storytelling but of truthful storytelling—narrating without leaving things out, or at least narrating in as truthful and inclusive a way as possible. If we are to be honest about the multidimensionality of the global church, its nuances and richness, its contradictions and frustrating realities, then the best way to do this is through an examination of a rich variety of stories and the use of a wide spectrum of storytelling styles. Thus my goal in this book is to mine a variety of narratives for their ecclesiological significance.

Some, like historical narratives, will have clear implications for ecclesiology: truth-telling about the continuous presence of nonimmigrant Hispanic Catholics in the continental United States, for example, which counters the narrative of an "American Catholicism" with only Northern European (and white-skinned) roots, or a Catholicism that is "emerging" as a Hispanic reality only because of recent migration of peoples instead of the absorption of many Hispanic Catholics into the United States during the nation's westward expansion. Other narratives, including the literary narratives, will have less obvious but no less important implications for the way we think about the church. Those narratives function in much the same way as my childhood understanding of my mom's protracted *cuéntame*—an invitation to listen in, to overhear. What might we overhear about the church's life, the church's story, in literary narratives, in art and music, in demographic presentations and ethnographic immersions?

The chapters that follow take a close look at a variety of narratives in search of ways to redirect ecclesiology from a top-down, deductive endeavor that has been the privileged paradigm of the hierarchical church to one that proceeds inductively from human experience. Because all human experience is embedded in cultural, geographic, and linguistic ways, the narratives in this text are not meant to be comprehensive but rather demonstrative. Moreover, they echo the idiosyncrasies of my own cultural, linguistic, and geographic context. The stories told and analyzed here reflect a particular perspective, one that was forged in a bilingual, Cuban-American exile community in Miami, filtered through years of education there and in the northeastern and midwestern United States. The book enacts a particular first-generation Cuban-American inflection, drawing on authors and theologians from the Antilles, as well as from other Latin American cultures. In short, the book rings true for me because it feels very Cuban-American. In writing it, I chose stories that I enjoyed, histories from which I learned about myself and my community. I traced demographics of people in my age group, and interviewed members of a lay community in my hometown.

As such, this book is a product of my perspective, and at the same time not only an invitation to others to bring their perspectives into dialogue with mine, but also an invitation to view other ecclesiological texts as necessarily perspectival rather than comprehensive or universal. Too often, especially in the northeastern United States, cultural understandings of Catholicism are mistaken for all-encompassing orthodoxies and orthopraxes. Only when we confront cultural understandings and contexts different from our customary reality is our own partial understanding of reality foregrounded. I learned this, embarrassingly, in my first week of college at Fordham University in the fall of 1994. I remember the perplexed look on people's faces when they didn't understand the Spanish words that would mix in with my conversation, or my strange struggles with prepositions and other constructions (I still say "ride bike," not "ride my bike"). I figured anyone who looked like me was Latina like me. It didn't occur to me that there were all kinds of "americanos"—Irish-, Italian-, Greek-, Polish-, German-Americans at school with me. It never crossed my mind that I was an anomaly to my classmates: "You don't LOOK Hispanic at all!" Thus began my education in the ways in which Latinx cultures operate in the United States, and how that differs—significantly— from how Latinx cultures operated and continue to operate in my home city of Miami. What this and many other experiences really revealed to me is the partial, imperfect quality of my understanding—a partiality and imperfection that is true of all persons, even and perhaps especially those who claim to be exempt from this aspect of the human condition.

This book sets out with an understanding that all knowledge and hermeneutics are incomplete and partial, that there are no comprehensive systems of understanding or acultural approaches to knowledge. It delves deeply into particularity, seeking out the universal in ways that only narrative and storytelling can convey. Stories draw us beyond our horizons of understanding, to paraphrase Hans-Georg Gadamer, into the world of the text, and force us to look again at our unexamined biases, preferences, and omissions. It is my hope that the stories highlighted in these pages reflect some particular experiences and expressions of Catholicism in the United States, so that others might be invited to interrogate their own cultural understandings of faith, and together we might build a mosaic befitting the variegated beauty of the people of God. By taking these stories into account, we can reorient ecclesiology away from a doctrinal starting point toward an experiential starting point. In so doing, we tell a truer story about the church.

The first chapter examines history as a narrative and looks carefully at the work of historians Timothy Matovina and David Badillo. Both scholars approach the history of Catholicism in America from a hemispheric, multiorigin perspective, rather than employing a narrative that focuses on Northern European immigration from the Northeast heading south and west. Taking seriously the presence of Hispanophone Roman Catholics in the South and West as part of the history of American Catholicism preserves the dangerous memory of these "other" Catholics and reminds ecclesiologists of the necessary variety that exists throughout the global church.

The next chapter turns to literary narrative as a resource for theology. Building on the methodological insights of Latina theologian Michelle Gonzalez-Maldonado, who advises Latinx theologians to "turn to literature as a resource for approaching and describing the faith and lives of Latino peoples,"[4] this chapter approaches a short story by Rosario Ferré and a triptych by Chicana artist Yolanda López as vehicles that allow ecclesiologists to "overhear" or grasp the sense of the faithful, that sacred intuition of faith mentioned in *Lumen Gentium* that belongs to the whole people of God. Then, using the seminal insights of Orlando Espín on the

---

4. Michelle Gonzalez, "Unearthing the Latino/a Imagination: Literature and Theology, Some Methodological Gestures," in *New Horizons in Hispanic/Latino Theology*, ed. Benjamin Valentín (Cleveland: Pilgrim Press, 2003), 119–37, 134.

relationship between popular Catholicism and the sense of the faithful, I point to how the work of these Latina artists subverts our understandings of Guadalupan devotion and hints at strains of popular Catholic Mariology that support the full human flourishing and self-determination of women.

Chapter 3 also looks at the impact of literary narratives on ecclesiology, but here we approach literature using Gonzalez-Maldonado's second methodological category of literature as theological source—approaching literature as theology, allowing it to spark methodological insights that help us see the church in a new light. Using a novel by Cuban author Daína Chaviano, this chapter explores Chaviano's text as an entry point for looking at the church as a palimpsest, where layers of history and practice are overlaid on one another and unearthed by theologians. Tasked with conveying the truth of the gospel in different ages and languages, theologians must attend to the cartography of ecclesial witness. We must be attentive to the ways the church has failed to be a vehicle of truth and mercy, and we must remedy this failure. Using the work of Ada María Isasi-Díaz on Latinas as multi-sites persons, this chapter looks at the church as a multi-sites reality that relies on unity built on understanding particularity, not forced uniformity.

Next we move away from literary narratives to a different sort of storytelling: demography. Tracing recent demographic trends points ecclesiologists toward the joys and hopes, griefs and anxieties of the people of God throughout the world, and so answers the invitation set forth in *Gaudium et Spes*. Demographic studies by Pew reveal a sharp rise in the number of persons who claim no religious affiliation, and the number of people who consider themselves Catholic has declined precipitously. Further investigation reveals that the rise in disaffiliation does not necessarily mean the decline of spiritual hunger or theistic belief, but rather a complex convergence of anti-institutionalism, perceived moral bankruptcy, and aging, increasingly obsolete ecclesial paradigms. Scholars such as Ken Davis, Hosffman Ospino, and David Badillo highlight how Latinx Catholics operate using other ecclesial paradigms, based in part on the Iberian roots of Latinx Catholicism. Features such as lay leadership and nonparish-based ecclesial communities, common in Latin America and among Latinx Catholics in the United States, might pave the way to new paradigms in U.S. Catholicism that take the concerns of the "nones" into account. The fourth chapter analyzes one nonparochial lay association of Catholics, the Agrupación Católica Universitaria (ACU), which was founded in Havana but survived expulsion from the island in the early 1960s and continues to thrive in the present. The ACU provides one example of how lay-led, extraparochial communities can coexist with and revitalize the fading model of the geographic parish.

The fifth and final chapter of this book gestures toward some features of a narrative ecclesiology in the third millennium. It looks closely at the International Theological Commission's 2014 document *"Sensus Fidei* in the Life of the Church," particularly at the notion of connaturality that undergirds the sense of the faithful. Connaturality is key not only to this supernatural instinct of the people of God, but to aesthetics, ethics, and hermeneutics. In dialogue with the work of Roberto Goizueta, this chapter examines how connaturality functions to attune us to the good, the true, and the beautiful, and how the notion of connaturality reorients our understandings of the unity and catholicity of the church.

A Note on Language

The writing of this book occurred over several years. During that time, awareness grew of the complexity of gender identity and the nonbinary character of the human gender landscape. In an effort to be as inclusive as possible, some scholars have adopted the use of the letter "x" in place of the masculine- or feminine-gendered nouns in Spanish, substituting, for example *hermanxs* for *hermanos/as*. A laudable linguistic move, this change strives to exclude no one from seeing themselves represented in writing and expression. Thus, Latinx has become more common than "Latino/a" or "Latin@" among some in the scholarly community. Throughout this text, I have used Latinx at times, but left Latina/o or Latino/a in place in others, depending on the cadence and sound of the sentence. While Latinx is ostensibly more inclusive, the ambiguous "x," as well as the question of pronunciation, makes it less appealing to me in some contexts. Importantly, my use of Latino/a, or Latinos/as, is not meant to be exclusionary of those with nonbinary gender identities. It is, instead, an aesthetic choice meant to either reflect the usage of the scholar on whose work I am building, or a matter of how the word looks and sounds in context. "Hispanic" and "hispanophone" also appear in the text, though Hispanic as a descriptor of Latinx communities has been mostly abandoned by Latinx theologians. These variations in naming exemplify how language evolves as context and understanding change, and they remind us of our incomplete and necessarily tentative attempts to capture the complex mystery of the divine–human encounter with language.

CHAPTER ONE

La increíble y triste historia
Historical Narratives
in Ecclesiology

The tradition manifests itself variously at various times:
sometimes by the mouth of the episcopacy, sometimes
by the doctors, sometimes by the people, sometimes
by liturgies, rites, ceremonies and customs, by events,
disputes, movements and all those other phenom-
ena which are comprised under the name of history.

—John Henry Newman
On Consulting the Faithful
in Matters of Doctrine

Narratives are a central feature of human experience. We
structure our self-awareness in narrative form. Our memories are oftentimes preserved in the form of stories we tell
and retell. The human capacity and affinity for storytelling
are a cornerstone of our identity and a reflection of divine
creativity. The stories we tell, therefore, carry much weight.
When reflecting on Christianity—a tradition founded on
biblical narratives and on the experience of encounter with
Jesus Christ, who was himself a teacher and storyteller—the
centrality of narrative cannot be denied. In his encounter
with the disciples on the road to Emmaus, Jesus recounts the

narrative of salvation to his friends, "opening up the scriptures to them," and thereby gives meaning to all they have witnessed in Jerusalem. This narrative element also holds true when thinking communally about the church that grew out of the encounter with Christ. Shared stories create community, just as memories, understood also as narratives, constitute personal identity. As such, narrative lies at the cornerstone of individual and group self-understandings, and these understandings include religious identity.

As Catholics, we believe that God's self-communication is not limited to a single text like those found in scripture, but rather takes the form of an event: the Incarnation, to which the scriptures are a witness. These revelatory events leading up to and following the Incarnation take place in history, making narrative(s) an appropriate medium for the process of understanding the events and eventually for the transmission of the events' significance. This accounts in part for the centrality of Tradition in Catholicism; the importance of the history of interpretation, the retelling of the Christian story in different languages and contexts, has historically been viewed as a good, as an essential part of the Catholic story. In an article in the journal *Ecclesiology* in 2008, John O'Brien defines the task of ecclesiology as "the project of giving a more systematic shape to what is striven for in [ecclesial or pastoral] praxis, and to the conversations between narratives that attempt to communicate and give meaning to it."[1]

An ecclesial example of this would be the Second Vatican Council. For those theologians who believe that Vatican II was marked by some discontinuity with the church and the ecclesiological approaches that preceded it, the revolutionary nature of the council does not reside merely in the documents that were promulgated by the council, but in the drama of the event itself—the biographies of those present, the meth-

---

1. John O'Brien, "Ecclesiology as Narrative," *Ecclesiology* 4 (2008): 150.

ods with which the bishops collaboratively wrote those documents, the debates about wording and content, and the players who shaped those debates. This dramatic unfolding in history is, for many, the "real story" of the council, not merely the set of documents it produced, which cannot be fully understood outside of this context.[2] Any understanding of Vatican II that only takes the final, promulgated documents into account is incomplete. The event reveals the story more fully, because we grasp reality as a series of events, and organize our understanding through narrative.

Because of this event-structure of reality and therefore also of the lives of the people of God who are the church, the form of storytelling, or narration, suits the objective of ecclesiology to systematize the praxis of the church. O'Brien states: "The basic *loci ecclesiologici* are the lives and actions of committed individuals and communities. Ecclesiology, present first of all in these lives as biography, is made accessible to the rest of us as a narrative."[3] In sharing our stories, Christians tell the truth about the church, make sense of its past, assess present doctrine and practice, and lay out the materials from which to construct an ecclesiology that is authentic and praxis based. This is a central insight of Latino/a theology—that the lives and practices of the people of God give rise to the genuine ecclesial story, and it is my claim that the systematization of these stories is the way to produce genu-

---

2. It is for this reason that I have found that one of the best texts for teaching the Second Vatican Council is *Vatican Council II* by Xavier Rynne [Francis X. Murphy] (Maryknoll, NY: Orbis Books, 1999). The "dispatches" genre of the text lends an urgency and an of-the-moment feeling to which students relate well. It bridges the distance between their historical context and that of the council. Writers such as Massimo Faggioli, William Madges, and Michael Daly also capture what they believe to be the "spirit" of the council in texts such as Madges and Daly, *Vatican II: Fifty Personal Stories* (Maryknoll, NY: Orbis Books, 2012), and Faggioli, *A Council for the Global Church: Receiving Vatican II in History* (Minneapolis: Fortress Press, 2015).

3. O'Brien, "Ecclesiology as Narrative," 153.

ine ecclesiological doctrine that is most faithful to the Christian message and to the people of God in history.[4]

The ecclesiological turn toward narrative has intensified in the last few decades, in part because the event of the Second Vatican Council changed the way theologians tell the story of the church in three ways. First, the council reoriented theology away from manuals and formulas and toward human experience as a starting point for theological reflection. As a result, the council renewed the ties between pastoral and systematic theology that many decades of neoscholasticism and academic theology had severed.[5] Second, in accordance with John XXIII's wishes, the council marked an *aggiornamento*, or an opening, in the church to new ideas and new voices, particularly voices from mission territories who had native-born bishops (not European transplants) representing them in the Sistine Chapel. This plurality of voices from Latin America, Africa, and Asia is a prime indicator that the global nature of the church begins to emerge at Vatican II. We see this also in the council's emphasis, especially in the Pastoral Constitution on the Church in the Modern World (*Gaudium et Spes*), on the poor, on the marginalized, and on those who suffer. In moving toward a more genuinely global narrative, the council changed ecclesiology in a third way, neatly encapsulated by feminist theologian Anne Carr: it moved away from static, idealized notions of perfection toward a more realistic appreciation of the messiness of the people of God in history.[6] Thus, instead of the church as a *societas perfecta*, *Lumen Gentium* speaks of the church primar-

---

4. For further thoughts on this, see my "*Hombres, Hembras, Hambres*: Narration, Correction, and the Work of Ecclesiology," *Journal of Hispanic/Latino Theology*, November 2011, http://latinotheology.org, 1–16.

5. O'Brien, "Ecclesiology as Narrative," 155.

6. Anne E. Carr, "Mary in the Mystery of the Church," in *Mary According to Women*, ed. Carol Frances Jegen BVM (Kansas City, MO: Sheed & Ward, 1985), 5–32, 27.

ily as a pilgrim people of God. *Dignitatis Humanae* nuanced the adage that outside the church there is no salvation with a robust defense of religious liberty and the importance of faith free from coercion. At the council, documents such as *Gaudium et Spes* were addressed to people of goodwill, not merely the church. Even *Lumen Gentium's* insistence that the Reign of God subsists in the Catholic Church, rather than an affirmation that these two realities are coextensive, points to the historicizing of theological doctrines and the radical (etymologically, "root based") entrance of the church into the messiness of fallible, imperfect, and incomplete human experience.

Despite this threefold reorientation of theology toward human experience, global reality, and historical ambiguity, the field of ecclesiology has been slow to embrace the methodological *aggiornamento* of the council. Nevertheless, recent ecclesiologies have adopted a more global perspective[7] and have moved away from overarching metanarratives that privilege stories from dominant Euro-American cultures and thereby marginalize narratives that disrupt these. Ultimately, ecclesiologists seem to have realized that in trying to tell a single story that encapsulates everyone's experience generally, only the experience of the powerful shines through. If, however, ecclesiology shifts toward narratives, and a dialogue among narratives, power relationships are laid bare, marginalized voices can be included, and through dialogue unity can emerge where uniformity was once imposed. In Gaillardetz's case, the search for an ecclesiology for a global church leads to a more plural, pastoral ecclesial picture that is true to the goals of the council. Still, a majority of ecclesiologists have tended to rely on the theoretical as a starting point. Some are structured around the marks of the church, selected seminal texts, or images, instead of the lived

---

7. See Richard Gaillardetz, *Ecclesiology for a Global Church: A People Called and Sent* (Maryknoll, NY: Orbis Books, 2008).

reality of the people of God.[8] Narratives can focus ecclesiology on the present moment without losing sight of the past, and can supplement a textual approach with more socio-historical insight that highlights the experience of those on the underside of history, and not necessarily history's victors. Thus, a narrative turn can truly reorient Catholic ecclesiology away from a methodology that begins with doctrinal formulations about the nature and mission of the church and toward a systematization of the praxis of the people of God.

A second important strain in contemporary ecclesiology, championed by John O'Brien and Ormond Rush, highlights the significance of narrative as the proper form of ecclesiology. Latino/a theology is particularly well suited to this ecclesiological method, because the work of Latino/a theologians has long focused, in terms of content, on the daily lives of the laity and the popular devotions in which they take part. From a methodological standpoint, the emphasis in Latino/a theology on interculturality and dialogue also seems well suited to a narrative or hermeneutical approach to the study of the church.

Latinx Theology and the Postconciliar Ecclesial Landscape

In the postconciliar era, ecclesiologists have, following trends in post–Vatican II theology, called for a turn to human experience as a locus for reflection on the church. Thinkers as diverse as Yves Congar, Edward Schillebeeckx, and Fernando Segovia have argued that ecclesiology should concern itself primarily with the experience of the people of God. For Schillebeeckx in particular, the arena of human activity served as a primary point of theological interest. In his "The Church with a Human Face," Schillebeeckx argues that ministry, the work of the church, is fundamen-

---

8. See McBrien's *Catholicism* or *The Church* for examples of thematic and historical approaches to ecclesiology.

tally socio-historic, and thus it is not reductionistic to look at the church through this lens. "There is no surplus of revelation behind or above the sociohistoric forms of ministry," he claims, against the "theological reductionism" that positions grace necessarily outside of history or alongside it.[9] Grace necessarily occurs in history; it is socio-historical, not ahistorical. Thus, to talk about the church as an otherworldly or alongside-the-world reality compartmentalizes the reality of grace in unproductive ways and relegates grace to a "supernatural" entity with little relation to the world it is meant to transform. Instead, Schilebeeckx advocates for a view of grace thoroughly enmeshed in history. Like the council that influenced him (and that he influenced), he calls thinkers to theologize human experience. In particular, Schillebeeckx advocated for theorizing human experience theologically through narrative. "Schillebeeckx highlights the revelatory power, the practical and critical effect, in narrative," writes Mary Catherine Hilkert. "Specifically, in the context of human suffering narrative has further power of retrieving the history of those whose lives have been forgotten, the invisible characters in history who've been dismissed as insignificant."[10] Narrative can make space for the marginalized, including marginalized epistemologies, oral traditions, overlooked communities. Furthermore, narrative allows what is most human about us—our failings, ambiguities, and contradictions—to come through and be part of the church's story. Narratives from a mix of cultures and generational groups in the church compose a mosaic, or tapestry, of the reality of the church. This is a far more fitting image given the church's relational function between God

9. Edward Schillebeeckx, *The Church with a Human Face* (New York: Crossroad, 1987), 5.

10. Mary Catherine Hilkert "The Discovery of the Living God," *The Praxis of Human Experience: An Introduction to the Theology of Edward Schillebeeckx*, ed. Robert Schreiter and Catherine Hilkert (New York: Harper & Row, 1989), 47.

and the world. A hermeneutics that recognizes the partiality of all knowledge and the necessity of a plurality of voices in the search for truth, even and especially ecclesiological truth, can aid in the collecting and understanding of the story mosaic.

In the U.S. context, one population repeatedly rendered insignificant until recently has been the Hispanic or Latino/a communities that reside in this country. They have long been taken for granted as obedient Catholics, and the richness of their culture and the intra-ethnic diversity of this people have been largely overlooked by theologians and commentators. Attention to Latinx Catholics, when paid, has focused on the emerging status of this community as the majority of the Roman Catholic Church in the United States, a distinction that has been met with surprise and with a tone of anticipation and preparation for this new reality. But the U.S. narrative of the "church of immigrants" overlooks the reality of longstanding Hispanic presence in the continental United States, as well as throughout the Americas, and paints the U.S. church in primarily Northern European categories, effectively erasing the multiple, diverse origins of Catholicism in the United States. After all, the first diocese in the Americas, San Juan in Puerto Rico (now a U.S. commonwealth, populated with U.S. citizens) was founded in 1511. The first church on the site of the present-day cathedral in Santa Fe was built in 1626. The reality of nonimmigrant Latinx Catholicism looms large in this nation.

Historian Timothy Matovina argues that American Catholicism is dominated by what he terms the "immigrant theory," the notion that Catholicism arrived in the United States when it was brought here by Northern European immigrants. In this theory, the Catholic population continues to be fed by a steady stream of Catholic immigration, more recently from the Global South. Thus, the story of "American Catholicism" tends to begin in the Northeast and spread south and west, ignoring the presence of Hispanic

Catholicism throughout what is now the continental United States. This immigrant theory ties into a nationalist narrative that conceals as much as it reveals.

The story of Hispanic Catholics in the United States subverts this immigrant/national narrative in favor of a more complex origin story, and a messier, more overlapping, and intertwined national religious history that acknowledges the reality of the U.S. conquest of some of Latin America while at the same time revealing the plural, diverse origins of Christianity itself. That is, the United States is merely one particular example of a longstanding Christian phenomenon of unity-in-diversity of practices, languages, and liturgical styles. The same could be said of the difference between the way Catholicism is practiced in Spain or in Germany. Though both are in Western Europe, and one would assume this confers a certain amount of overlap, the effusive processions of *Semana Santa* in Seville are unique but no less related to the central mystery of Easter celebrated by the church universal. Similarly, worship in parts of southern Germany differs from that of some practices in the more reserved northern parts of the country.

So too, uncovering the Latinx Catholic historical narrative unsettles the so-called American story in order to situate it within the broader context of the Latin American Catholic story, and complicates the self-image of U.S. Catholics as primarily an Anglo-European church. In place of the immigrant theory, Matovina proposes the "hemispheric view," a multilocal origin story for American Catholicism, with roots in northern and southern Europe (Germany and Ireland, as well as Spain, Italy, and Portugal) and with originating points on this continent not only in Maryland but also in New Mexico, not merely in Philadelphia but in Florida as well. The U.S. church, then, becomes pan-American, not merely North American and still less generically "American." Latino Catholics have been part of U.S. history since before there was a United States to analyze. The reality of nonimmigrant Hispanic Catholics is one with which we must contend if we are to tell true stories about the roots of the U.S. church.

Richard Gaillardetz notes that "the oneness of the faith is often discovered only by first courageously attending to what manifests itself as foreign or different."[11] For the church in the United States, unfortunately, some of what is manifest as foreign is in fact part of the long history of Catholicism on this continent, namely, the liturgical practices and popular devotions of U.S. Latinos and Latinas. As a result, the story of American Catholicism benefits greatly from the work of U.S. Latino/a theology, which for the better part of the last forty years has been dedicated to theorizing the complex identities, practices, and everyday lives of Latino/a Catholics in the United States.[12]

Latinx theology is particularly well suited to a narrative turn in ecclesiology for genealogical, methodological, and thematic reasons. First, Latinx theology has roots in the *Encuentro* meetings of pastoral ministers that grew out of the call to collegiality and synodality in the Second Vatican Council. In an effort to have input into the pastoral plan for Hispanics in the United States, pastoral ministers, clergy, and other experts came together periodically beginning in 1972 in a series of *Encuentros*, meetings that fueled not only the U.S. bishops' pastoral planning for Hispanic Catholics but also the theological and pastoral imaginations of these Catholics. As a result, Latino/a theology as a discipline has at its origin a desire to bridge the pastoral and the systematic— a desire evidenced in the documents of the *Encuentros* that echo the aims of Vatican II, and that a narrative turn can

---

11. Richard Gaillardetz, *Ecclesiology for a Global Church: A People Called and Sent* (Maryknoll, NY: Orbis Books, 2008), 35.

12. On this, see especially Eduardo Fernandez S.J., *La Cosecha: Harvesting Contemporary United States Hispanic Theology (1972–1988)* (Collegeville, MN: Michael Glazier, 2000).

facilitate. For O'Brien, "what the church is cannot be simply found . . . within a doctrinal system. What Church is unfolds in and through the drama of salvation mediated in lives of engaged individuals and communities."[13] The *Encuentros*, which gathered pastoral ministers, clergy, and theologians, bridged the so-called gap between the (nonspecific, non-experiential) doctrinal realm and the pastoral realm, and in the process brought forth a new way of doing theology of, by, and for Latinx communities.

Second, and as a corollary to this alliance between the pastoral and the systematic, Latinx theology strives to be methodologically collaborative, pioneering a style of theology known as *teología en conjunto*, which implies not merely collaboration but mutually respectful critique and dialogue as theological methodology. A foundational element of Latinx theology is this view of thinking as a collaborative endeavor, done from specific communities and attempting to allow the marginalized voices of these communities to speak, as in the work of Ada María Isasi-Díaz, who viewed her theological task as one of midwifery. But even in the realm that would be considered strictly scholarly, the Academy of Catholic Hispanic Theologians of the United States does things a bit differently, opting for a colloquium that centers on conversation and mutual critique of previously distributed work, rather than the reading of scholarly papers one finds at other academic conferences. This is not a function of ACHTUS's relatively small numbers (the society has approximately 250 to 300 members) but instead a methodological choice that views collaboration as key to theological insight. Dialogue among differing narratives is an essential feature of this *teología en conjunto*. A further methodological strength for Latinx theology in this vein is its intercultural nature, and the habit many Latino/a theologians have of negotiating (personally and professionally) multicultural and intercultural spaces.

---

13. O'Brien, "Ecclesiology as Narrative," 148–65, 151.

This is an invaluable skill for ecclesiology, as well as narrativity, which lends itself to intercultural dialogue, a critical skill in a global church.

Lastly, Latinx theologies mesh thematically with narrative ecclesiology because they take seriously the everyday lives of the laity, the importance of popular religious practices, and consequently the role of women in creating and preserving Catholic identity. Two of the most important thematic contributions to mainstream theology pioneered by Latinx theologians are an emphasis on everyday life—the sacredness of *lo cotidiano*—and a sustained focus on popular religious practices that permeate Latinx communities in the United States and abroad. This focus on specific, daily reality as a site of grace and as a locus of theological reflection easily lends itself to narrative as a form that can convey the intricacies of individual, graced lives. In the process of emphasizing popular religion and *lo cotidiano*, a third, vital awareness emerged: the prominence of Hispanic women in religious roles within and outside the home. Frequently sought out as sources of blessing and healing, older women in particular serve as the religious backbone of families, communities, and churches. Lifting up these narratives is key to elaborating an ecclesiology for the twenty-first century.

The *Encuentros* and Latinx Theology's Pastoral-Systematic Roots

In the wake of the collegial and synodal spirit emerging from Vatican II, national bishops' conferences strengthened in the 1970s, establishing themselves in some cases as the local overseeing bodies that the council had imagined in *Lumen Gentium*. Beginning in 1972, leaders in the field of Hispanic pastoral ministry gathered periodically from across the United States to make the needs and priorities of their communities known to the U.S. bishops in the hopes of helping to shape the way the Hispanic communities in the United States were served by the church. These meetings, termed *Encuentros* (encounters), continue to the present day, as Hispanic faith leaders prepare for the fifth *Encuentro* in 2018. As the process of planning and organizing the meetings matured, particularly in the second and third *Encuentros*, these summits had an enormous impact in how the U.S. hierarchy approached Hispanic pastoral ministry, and for the first time gave U.S. Latinos and Latinas a voice in their ecclesial destinies. The *Encuentros* also pioneered a theological method of workshopping and collaboration that Latino/a theologians continue to use today. Many *Encuentro* participants used the platforms offered them at the meetings to the fullest, collaborating on documents that would eventually become pastoral plans for the United States Conference of Catholic Bishops (in 1987).

Historical analyses of the *Encuentros* such as Matovina's and a dissertation by Luis Tampe S.J. are crucial to understanding the *Encuentros'* impact, but what is significant for this study are the participatory nature of the meetings and the focus on grassroots solutions and collaborative methods of proposing these solutions. Also important here is the postconciliar emphasis on reading the Hispanic presence in the U.S. church as a sign of the times and, consequently, the attempt to respond to this reality in light of the gospel. For example, Tampe's recently completed dissertation on the *Encuentro* process looks at each meeting in detail and analyzes the historical and ecclesiological themes flowing from each gathering.[14] The *Encuentros* brought together leaders in Latinx ministry—clergy and lay, academic and pastoral—and each *Encuentro* produced a series of recommendations for the church as a whole to meet the needs of the growing numbers of Hispanic Catholics in the U.S. church. Thus, the meetings themselves had as a goal to produce better pastoral

---

14. Luis Tampe S.J., "Encuentro Nacional Hispano de Pastoral (1972–1985): An Historical and Ecclesiological Analysis" (Ph.D. thesis, Catholic University of America, 2014).

outcomes, specifically in the world of Catholic Hispanic ministry.

The *Encuentro* gatherings are theologically significant because they put into practice the participative and collaborative processes of church governance endorsed by Vatican II, emulated by the Latin American Bishops' Conference (CELAM) at Medellín, and echoed by contemporary systematic theologians. The *Encuentros* were rooted in pastoral practice, but included the presence of theologians (like Virgilio Elizondo, one of the founders of U.S. Latino/a theology), clergy, and community organizers who helped shape the agenda and the outcomes. As collaborative processes, the *Encuentros* modeled the *en conjunto* methodology outlined by the Latin American bishops at Medellín. For Matovina, the second *Encuentro* was even more successful than the first, with an overwhelming majority of lay participants and observers, along with the eight Hispanic bishops serving in the United States at the time.[15]

> Certainly the most ambitious accomplishment of the Second Encuentro was the extensive consultation beginning in small community gatherings that made the process a learning experience for thousands of Hispanic Catholics and an opportunity for them to voice their concerns to their church leaders and coreligionists. Consequently, whereas the pastoral insights articulated in the First Encuentro were deepened rather than redirected in the Second Encuentro, the latter's conclusions had the weight of emerging from a process encompassing a wide group of grassroots Hispanic Catholics rather than the more elite leadership group of its predecessor.[16]

---

15. Timothy Matovina, *Latino Catholicism: Transformation in America's Largest Church* (Princeton, NJ: Princeton University Press, 2012), 80.

16. Ibid., 82.

The workshop methodology and wide net of participation from diverse communities all over the Spanish-speaking parishes of the United States had a profound effect on U.S. Latino/a theology that would emerge after the first *Encuentro* meeting in 1972. From its foundation in 1988, the Academy of Catholic Hispanic Theologians of the United States, the first and only theological body for U.S. Catholic Latino/a theologians, reflected the workshop methodology of the *Encuentros* in its meetings. Latinx theology continues to affirm a close tie between pastoral and systematic theology, in part through its emphasis on the daily life of the laity. These methodological and thematic characteristics found in U.S. Latino/a theology can be traced to the *Encuentro* processes, with their emphasis on a wide net of participation, reporting from lay leaders who were on the ground working in the communities, and contextualizing conversations between theologians, clergy, and pastoral leaders. In Latinx theologies, these seeds have borne fruit in methodological collaboration/*conjunto,* on practical solutions for pastoral issues facing Hispanics, and on the intra-Hispanic diversity and intercultural reality that is a hallmark of U.S. Latino/a identity.

Methodological *Latinidad*:
Collaboration and Interculturality

A central theme of the *Encuentros* was the inherently multicultural reality of the Hispanic community in the United States. The idea that Hispanic culture exists in the singular (i.e., instead of "cultures") is a fantasy born of dismissiveness or ignorance on the part of the dominant cultures of the United States. Even the term "Hispanic," coined by the U.S. Census office to count Spanish-speaking persons of Latin American or Spanish descent living in the United States, is viewed by many as an unwelcome and imposed category that obscures more than it reveals about the vastly different cultures that make up the Spanish-speaking world. Delegates to the second *Encuentro* stressed that the church should "keep in mind the sensitivities and historical circumstances of the different communities which compose the Hispanic mosaic in the United States. . . ."[17]

The language of "mosaic" emphasizes the real and profound differences in race, class, migratory status, and social standing represented in the different Spanish-speaking communities of the United States. The experience of the Cuban-American exile community in South Florida or New Jersey differs enormously from Chicanos in Texas or Southern California, which in turn differs from the experience of Salvadorans in Washington, DC, or Venezuelans or Puerto Ricans or Dominicans in the northeastern United States.

A community's circumstances of migration serve as one example. Cubans—who identify themselves as exiles and were overwhelmingly white and middle- to upper-class in the initial migration to the United States in the 1950s and '60s—simply do not have the same experience as, say, Puerto Ricans or Dominicans who migrated to the Northeast in dire economic circumstances, or as Mexican American families whose residence in the southwestern United States predates the Treaty of Guadalupe Hidalgo, which annexed much of the western and southwestern parts of the mainland, including all of California, most of New Mexico and Arizona, and parts of Nevada, Colorado, and Wyoming. One cannot compare the experience of crossing the border to that of having the borders of a country cross your home, making you a nonimmigrant foreigner in the land of your birth. These differences hold true in a variety of instances, from linguistic dialects to cultural norms to religious preferences.

The racial and cultural mixture that gave rise to what would become "Hispanics" in the United States is a reality that U.S. Latinx theologians have analyzed for decades.

---

17. Secretariat for Hispanic Affairs/National Conference of Catholic Bishops, *Proceedings of the II Encuentro* (Washington, DC: Secretariat for Hispanic Affairs, 1978), 68–69.

From its inception, U.S. Latinx theology has used the category of *mestizaje* to describe the multiple racial and cultural origins of some Hispanic communities, to which scholars such as Michelle Gonzalez have added the category of *mulatez*, denoting the mixture of Spanish and African blood that typifies a variety of Latin American and Hispanic communities in Latin America and especially in the Caribbean.[18] The people that resulted from the violent confrontations of European conquistadors with the indigenous inhabitants of the Americas and the Caribbean, and subsequently from the confrontations of these communities with enslaved Africans, is necessarily intercultural, forged by *mestizaje* and *mulatez*. It is racially, ethnically, linguistically, and religiously plural, and Latinx theologians as a group have wished to celebrate and interrogate this plurality, not erase it.

At the same time, Latinos/as in the United States distinguish themselves from Latin Americans living elsewhere. Thus there exists a sense of in-betweenness that characterizes the lives of U.S. Hispanics. Matovina cites the founding documents of the Mexican American Cultural Center (MACC) in San Antonio, Texas, which note that Hispanics are "well aware that we are not typical white Anglo-Saxon middle class North Americans but we also became critically conscious that we were not the same as Mexicans living in Mexico or Latin Americans in Latin America."[19] The unique situation of Hispanic Catholics as a multiracial, multiethnic, multicultural majority-minority group calls for a unique approach to theology and ministry. What, then, could it mean to do theology in a Latino/a way, or *latinamente*?

For Mexican-American feminist theologian María Pilar

---

18. *Mestizaje* is not a noncontested category, however. For some contemporary challenges to this notion, see Nestor Medina, *Mestizaje: Remapping Race, Culture, and Faith in Latina/o Catholicism* (Maryknoll, NY: Orbis Books, 2009).

19. MACC Founding Documents, cited in Matovina, *Latino Catholicism*, 75.

Aquino, the answer is that U.S. Latino/a theology is necessarily intercultural and recognizes, from its inception, that no culture or thought system has a monopoly on the truth, but rather that the fullest truth can be gleaned only through dialogue among diverse groups with varying approaches and epistemological presuppositions.[20] She writes:

> This is a theology born within a reality where a number of religious traditions and several theological formulations converge. European, Latin American, European American, Afro-Latin and African American, American, Native American, and feminist traditions and elaborations have been welcome and critically embraced. And yet, U.S. Latino/a theology acquired its own personality because its [intercultural] cradle lies within the concrete and complex reality of the Latino/a communities of the United States, which in turn constitute an intercultural community.[21]

From the intercultural reality of the plural identities that make up Hispanic communities in the United States arise a variety of epistemological and theological perspectives, and these in turn are in dialogue with the prevailing theological, philosophical, and epistemological trends in the dominant and nondominant cultures that make up the U.S. academy. Latino/a theology is simultaneously a narrative of liberation (of oppressed and marginalized Hispanic persons in the United States) and one of resistance to the brute forces of assimilation and the erasure of difference that tend to dominate in U.S. culture. Too often, assimilation or the melting-pot mentality has meant the eradication of difference, or more accurately, a deliberate erasing or ignoring of differences that go against

---

20. María Pilar Aquino, "Theological Method in U.S. Latino/a Theology," in *From the Heart of Our People* (Maryknoll, NY: Orbis Books, 1999), 6–48.

21. Ibid., 24–25.

the dominant culture's notions of what is true, rational, good, or holy. Latinx theologians stand firmly against this, arguing that it is precisely in lifting up nondominant notions of rationality, of beauty, and of holiness that the richness of reality, which is necessarily intercultural, is revealed.

Against this pressure to overlook and eradicate difference, Latinx theology draws near to its life-giving source: the praxis of the people of God, as evidenced in popular religious practices and daily life. Although these practices and lives are necessarily disparate and diverse, Latinx theology seeks to delve deeply into the particularity of human experience, and this methodological choice to emphasize the real faith of the real church, as Orlando Espín has referred to popular Catholicism, pays off. After all, as both Virgilio Elizondo and Roberto Goizueta have noted, it is only in delving deep into particularity that true universal import is revealed. Elizondo writes that "the more universal one tries to be, the less one has to offer to others. Conversely, the more particular a thought is, the more its universal implications become evident."[22] Or, as Goizueta puts it, "The scandal of U.S. Hispanic popular Catholicism to both the modern and the postmodern scholar is precisely that, for us, these practices reveal universal, indeed cosmological truth—that, therefore, is normative for everyone. Guadalupe is meaningful for us because it is true for everyone—and it is true for everyone because it is meaningful for us."[23] This emphasis on particularity as revealed in popular Catholic practice echoes the Second Vatican Council's turn to human experience and history; it accounts for the intercultural reality that is *latinidad*, and it reveals with particular poignancy the universal truth of God's engagement with a particular set of communities in history—and what is ecclesiology if not the

---

22. Virgilio Elizondo, *Irruption of the Third World*, cited in Aquino, "Theological Method," 25.

23. Goizueta, *Caminemos con Jesús*, 155.

story of that engagement? What is the church if not the community that responds to that engagement?

People and Practice: Thematic Resonances Between Latinx Theology and Narrative Ecclesiology

The work of Latinx theologians, while not producing an explicit, systematic ecclesiology, nevertheless has taken up a variety of themes central to the task of ecclesiology including the following: Tradition, the sense of the faithful, the sacredness of everyday life, and the role of women in transmitting and preserving faith. Orlando Espín's seminal work on popular Catholicism and popular religious devotion in U.S. Hispanic communities serves as the cornerstone of any attempt to think ecclesiologically about Latinx theological themes. Espín's reflections on popular religiosity and popular devotions in the U.S. context reveal a powerful narrative of what he calls "the real faith of the real church." Noting that the majority of Catholics have always been the lay poor, Espín avers that postconciliar theology has been "unsuccessful in theologizing the laity" at all.[24] Ecclesiology, as the narrative of the people of God in history, has the capacity to fill that void, and Espín's insights about popular Catholicism provide important context for bridging the gap between idealized categories like "Tradition" or *"sensus fidelium"* and the lived religion of large numbers of Catholics.

In a 1988 session at the annual meeting of the Catholic Theological Society of America, Sixto Garcia identified popular religiosity as

> the set of experiences, beliefs, and rituals which more or less peripheral groups create, assume, and develop within concrete sociocultural and historical contexts and as a response to these contexts, and which to a greater or lesser degree distance themselves (super-

---

24. Espín, *Faith of the People*, 4.

ficially or substantively) from what is recognized as normative by church and society, striving (through rituals, experiences, and beliefs) to find an access to God and salvation which they feel they cannot find in what the church and society present as normative.[25]

Home altars, processions, festivals, public reenactments of biblical scenes; all form part of the Catholic life of millions of Latin Americans and Latinos/as in the United States. Latino/a Catholic religiosity is rooted in part in the Iberian Catholicism that was brought to the Americas, which privileged local devotions over the official, parish-centered practices that became common in Europe much later. This faith was rural, had sparse access to clergy, and even less access to the centralizing efforts of the Tridentine and post-Tridentine period.

Thus, the devotionalism that the conquistadors and their companions brought to the Americas took hold in new localities, many of which were already considered sacred by indigenous communities. In this way, Iberian Catholicism inculturated itself among indigenous traditions and, later, African religiosities as well. At times in the history of the church this devotional strain in Latino/a Catholicism has been viewed as backward or an embarrassment, a vestige of superstition that must be overcome with proper catechesis. Espín, on the contrary, privileges the faith of the people, their major festivals and their private devotions, as a *locus theologicus*, a site where theological reflection can and must happen. After all, he notes, the majority of Roman Catholics are and have always been the lay poor—why would we assume that God is not at work in their faith? If the adage *lex orandi lex credendi* (the law of prayer is the law of belief—that is, the way people pray reflects what they believe) has any truth, then theologians must examine the public and private

---

25. Sixto Garcia, Address to Catholic Theological Society of America in Allan Deck, *Frontiers of Hispanic Theology in the United States* (Maryknoll, NY: Orbis Books, 1992), 90.

prayer lives of their communities in order to theologize from a genuine understanding of the faith of the people.

Two themes of ecclesiological import emerge from a study of popular religious practices, and popular Catholicism in particular. First, as Espín rightly points out, popular Catholicism is a bearer of tradition. Dominant theological epistemologies tend to privilege texts as the sole record of the vast Tradition that Vatican II upheld as a counterpart to scripture in revelation. But texts do not tell the whole story, particularly the story of the poor, the marginalized, or the conquered. To get at the real faith of this large portion of the church, one must look at popular Catholicism and devotions. This is in keeping with the methodology of Latinx theology, which points out that epistemological presuppositions, like any knowledge, are culturally bound, and what counts as rational is in large part decided by the culture that is in power at the time. Thus, different forms of rationality must be explored in the intercultural dialogue envisioned by María Pilar Aquino and others as the method of Latino/a theology. With this in mind, it makes sense that popular religious practices should be considered alongside theological texts as bearers of tradition, given that they, too, communicate the understanding of the faith held by Catholic Christians in a particular context. Longstanding practices, like pilgrimages, *posadas*, or public *via crucis* clearly convey a sense of the faith and resonate with Latinos/as across generations, migrations, and other changing circumstances.

Women, Popular Religion, and the Sense of the Faithful

The ecclesiological term most helpful in referring to this faith of the people is the *sensus fidei*, the elusive category mentioned in *Lumen Gentium* 6 as contributing to the church's inerrancy: "the whole people of God . . . cannot err in matters of belief." Popular religion, while not completely coextensive with the *sensus fidei*, is nevertheless a bearer of the *sensus fidei*.

It contextualizes and lives out (and therefore contributes to) doctrines and beliefs such as the role of Mary, the miracle of the Incarnation (in the *posadas*), the paschal mystery (in the *via crucis*), and others. Espín is careful to stress that the *sensus fidelium*[26] and popular Catholicism are not synonymous: the *sensus fidelium* exists as an intuition, and popular devotions are expressions of these intuitions that require interpretation. But the work of interpretation should not displace the centrality of popular religious practices for the Latino/a Catholic experience. For Sixto Garcia, popular religious practices "constitute a popular hermeneutics."[27] Instead, these practices should serve as a cornerstone of theology, an expression of the *sensus fidelium*, and an avenue for transmitting the faith—a bearer of tradition. Because of this, popular religiosity is essential to ecclesiology, but it is rarely given the attention it merits.

One remarkable characteristic of popular Catholicism is the consistency with which it is practiced across different Latino/a communities.[28] It is evident in cities and towns, in

---

26. Espín utilizes the term *sensus fidelium* to mean the faithful intuition of a plurality of Catholics who engage in popular Catholicism and popular devotional practices. I use the term *sensus fidei* in keeping with the definitions set out by the International Theological Commission distinguishing between the *sensus fidei fidelis* and the *sensus fidei fidelium*, where the former refers to a Catholic's personal intuition of faith and the latter to the church's communal intuition. Since the ITC distinguishes these as a matter of number and not materially different (both are intuitions, both are nondiscursive, both must be discerned) I am keeping Espín's language of *fidelium* with the understanding that he means the intuition of faith exercised by believers individually and communally in culturally bound ways. More will be said about the ITC's "*Sensus Fidei* in the Life of the Church (2014)" in chapter 5.

27. Ibid., 91.

28. Neither is popular Catholicism limited to communities with Latin American roots. See Robert Orsi, *The Madonna of 115th Street: Faith and Community in Italian Harlem, 1880–1950* (New Haven: Yale University Press, 1985), for many examples of Italian popular Catholicism in New York City.

literature and television, in music and art. From the music of Celina and Rutilio, a duet in 1950s Cuba whose hits included "Virgen del Cobre" and "Santa Barbara," to a 1993 telenovela entitled "Guadalupe" and starring famed Mexican telenovela actress Adela Noriega produced by Televisa, a major Mexican media conglomerate, popular Catholicism permeates the popular culture of Hispanic communities. Chicago's Pilsen neighborhood celebrates a public *via crucis* in Spanish every Good Friday, bringing popular Catholicism to the streets of the Midwest. For marginalized communities like many Latino/a communities in the United States, who were frequently underserved by the church with few Spanish-speaking clergy and little receptivity to their pastoral needs, popular Catholicism provided (and in many cases continues to provide) a lifeline to faith and spiritual sustenance. Its widespread nature indicates that for many, popular Catholicism is part of their everyday reality, whether through curating home altars, celebrating yearly at gravesides on the Day of the Dead, or participating in Marian or other saints' processions. Though they occur outside the parish, these practices are no less central to faith. Neither do they detract from major celebrations such as the Eucharist. Instead, extra-parochial religious practices create community that moves beyond the geographic (and often, unwelcoming) boundaries of the parish and reinforce religious and cultural identity. Like the centrality of popular devotions for understanding the *sensus fidelium* or for making our notion of tradition more robust, these practices encourage Latino/a theologians to reflect on another major ecclesiological theme, the sacredness of everyday life, or *lo cotidiano*.

Theorizing on the importance of everyday life owes much to feminist liberation movements that focused on women's experience, often largely confined to the home and ignored as insignificant. Since the days of "the personal is political," however, theologians have taken up the task of reflecting on the ordinary, everyday character of grace. In Latino/a theology, this has been a particular strength of Latina and *mujerista* theologians.[29] Aquino writes: "It is in daily life where revelation occurs. We have no other place but *lo cotidiano* to welcome the living Word of God or to respond to it in faith. The faith of the people as lived and expressed in popular Catholicism happens within the dynamics of everyday existence."[30] Of particular import for ecclesiology is the notion that grace occurs in the everyday, and that discipleship, the pilgrimage of the people of God, does not consist of a series of dramatic, extrahistorical moments but rather in humble sacred moments that take place in the business of life. Latina theologians in particular have stressed the importance of *lo cotidiano*, or the everyday, ordinary lives of Christians as a counterpoint to mainstream/dominant theologies' overreliance on the experience (and texts) of Euro-American males. If Latina religiosity is narrated in everyday life, then that story should form part of the church's story, particularly since Latinas are widely regarded as the most influential religious actors in Hispanic families and, increasingly, in parishes and lay movements.

Indeed, the centrality of women in Latinx Catholicism cannot be overstated. This, too, is an important consideration for any ecclesiology in the third millennium. Latinx theologians consistently highlight the indispensability of mothers, grandmothers, aunts, and others as the primary agents of catechesis and traditioning across Hispanic communities. Scholars emphasize the role of the *abuelita* in passing on faith to her grandchildren or of the aunts, cousins, or *comadres* (for they need not be biologically related) in church membership and in leadership roles in communal religious

---

29. Not all Latina theologians consider themselves mujerista. This is a term coined by Ada María Isasi-Díaz to denote a kind of feminist praxis that is liberative and committed to theorizing the concrete lives of Latinas. See her *Mujerista Theology: A Theology for the Twenty-First Century* (Maryknoll, NY: Orbis Books, 1996).

30. Aquino, "Theological Method," 39.

devotions. Women offer blessings, lead processions in the public sphere, and inculcate religious and moral teachings in the private sphere. Many, if not most Latinos and Latinas (myself and my children included) learned to pray from their grandmothers. Espín notes:

> The ministers of Latino Catholicism are primarily the older women. They are deemed wiser and usually in possession of greater personal and spiritual depth than the men. Women are the center and pillars of the families and Latino popular Catholicism is definitely woman-emphatic. It is no exaggeration to say that older women are our people's cultural and religious herme-neuts.[31]

Though one could make the case that antifeminism and misogyny are rampant in Hispanic cultures (as they are in other cultures), it cannot be denied that in the religious sphere, Latinas are profoundly influential and respected as such. They do not hold these respected positions as sub-par alternatives to male leadership, but rather as a matter of course, as a matter of their centrality to families, communities, and societies. This is a lesson Latino/a theology and praxis can bring to ecclesiology as a whole.

Latinx Ecclesiological Inroads

Popular Catholicism, though key, is not the only important contribution to Latino/a theology's ecclesial output. Think-ers like Gary Riebe-Estrella have proffered incisive ecclesial analysis by making an anthropological turn to the Latino/a as a socially constituted subject. With Espín's popular-devotional insight, theological anthropology represents another fruitful, narrative turn in Latino/a theology. Espín's sustained analysis of popular religion and the faith of the

---

31. Espín, *Faith of the People*, 4.

marginalized and excluded successfully theologizes the faith of the majority of the church, whose experience and praxis had been deemed irrelevant to mainstream theological discourse. By retrieving and highlighting popular religion, devotions, and practices, Espín is able to foreground classical theological themes like the *sensus fidelium,* the notion of Tradition, the interplay of sin and grace as they manifest in the Latino/a communities from whose perspective he writes.

Like Espín, Riebe-Estrella seeks to ground his theology in concrete human experience. Thus his ecclesiology is founded on an anthropological insight: that the notion of "pueblo" (meaning people as well as town) signifies Latina/o notions of church exceptionally well because of the sociocentric anthropology of Latinos. In Latina/o cultures, "the fundamental unit of society is envisioned as a group, primarily the family."[32] Over against dominant Euro-American models of culture, which he classifies as "egocentric-contractual," Riebe posits a vision of Latino/a church and culture that is founded on personal identity that is forged in preset involuntary relationships. This relational anthropology in turn forms a basis for a "pueblo" ecclesiology where the network of human relationships is not something one enters into (and consequently can leave) after free consideration, but instead, like a family, where relationships are a given, constitutive of selfhood. "Being church is not something that needs to be constructed but something which flows naturally out of our relationships."[33] For Latino Catholics, then, the council's idea of the church as people of God is most fitting, and fruitful, prompting the church to ground the notion of peoplehood not in some idealized symbolic past (the "new Israel"), but in concrete communities that journey in discipleship today.

To do this, Riebe suggests that a shift in methodology is imperative. Just as the council turned toward human

---

32. Riebe-Estrella, "Pueblo and Church," 173.
33. Ibid., 182.

experience, Riebe, Espín, Aquino, and others call for a methodological conversion in ecclesiology, ushered in by an epistemological dialogue. An eyewitness account is incomplete without multiple witnesses, and in a similar way, Latino/a theologians contend that it is only through dialogue and collaboration between and among theological constituencies that a genuine picture of the church can come about. The dearth of Hispanic ecclesiology, decried by every major figure in Latino/a theology, has more to do with the need for a methodological shift away from deductive "applied" theology and more toward an inductive, narrative-based ecclesiology.[34] This text is a step in that direction. It is my contention that a shift toward narrative as source and resource for ecclesiology is precisely the methodological shift that is called for. Not only personal narratives or devotional narratives, though those are important, but literary narratives, ethnographic narrative, demographic narratives, and more can serve as ecclesiological guideposts for the Catholic Church in the third millennium.

If, as John O'Brien states, the basic loci of ecclesiology are the lives of committed Catholics, then no theological school has theorized more extensively on this ecclesiological site than Latino/a theology. Its relentless commitment to the concrete, historical, context-interdependent lives of Latino/as across the United States, to their prayers and practices, their liturgies, and their everyday lives gathers up the material for a compelling story of the people of God.

It is up to a second generation of theologians to gather these stories, to put them in conversation with narratives from other communities espousing other epistemologies and methods, in an effort to finally make the turn to human

---

34. On the distinction between deductive, applied theology, and Latinx approaches to ecclesiology, see Gary Riebe-Estrella, "Catholic Ecclesiology," in *The Wiley Blackwell Companion to Latina/o Theology*, ed. Orlando Espín (West Sussex, UK: John Wiley & Sons, 2015), 191–98.

experience so convincingly ushered in by *Gaudium et Spes* and *Lumen Gentium*. Latinx theology's rootedness in the *Encuentro* process, a hybrid of pastoral and systematic theology, bears fruit in a theology that prizes devotional practice, everyday life, and the leadership of women of faith. Socially, economically, and methodologically intercultural, Latino theologians draw on their explorations of forging identity through multiple violent encounters (resulting in a mestizo race) to a galvanizing intercultural dialogue meant to build alliances to fight injustice. By modeling interculturality and dialogue among the different ethnic, racial, class, and social constituencies that make up the umbrella categories of "Hispanic" and "Latino/a," this theological discourse exemplifies a way forward toward the global church ushered in at the Second Vatican Council but yet to be realized in the church's policy, practices, and ecclesiological self understanding.

Through an examination of a variety of narratives, the chapters that follow will make an attempt at the methodological shift in ecclesiology advocated by Latino/a theologians. Literary, ethnographic, historical narratives all tell partial stories that when woven together have the potential to reveal the church's story in its particular, and therefore universally relevant, contours with regard to the Latino/a community. As Ormond Rush reminds us echoing Paul Ricoeur, "there is a narrative quality to experience. The content of faith is understood in terms of one's unique life story."[35] By analyzing various takes on the life stories of Latinos/as, an interdisciplinary narrative ecclesiology will highlight the interculturality of the Christian tradition, bring the *sensus fidei* to the fore as a central category in ecclesiology, and theologize the laity as the majority and the prime subjects of ecclesial experience and action (and not merely its objects).

---

35. Ormond Rush, "Sensus Fidei: Faith 'Making Sense' of Revelation," *Theological Studies* 62 (May 2001): 231–61.

CHAPTER TWO

Más que cuentos
Literary Narrative as
Resource for Ecclesiology

There is no doubt fiction makes a better job of the truth.
—Doris Lessing, *Under My Skin*

This chapter takes its title from a Latin American warning against rumor, a caution that something is *nada más que cuentos*, that is, "nothing more than stories." It warns us not to believe "the hype," because it is nothing more than tales, or *cuentos*. A plausible alternative title would have used *vivir del cuento*, which denotes the state of living off of a fundamental unreality—stories, not truth. Our cultural obsession with data-driven analysis often decries the perils of "anecdata" or personal accounts as less reliable than wide-ranging studies and repeatable experiments, and this criterion holds true in many fields. But Christianity would not survive or even exist without stories. Narratives are, as argued earlier, the lifeblood of Christianity—grounded as it is in the story of the Incarnation, of God-with-us, and of Jesus's salvific activity on earth, including the Resurrection. The title of this chapter, then, is in fact a reversal—stories and storytelling actually present and re-present more than "just stories," particularly if one looks at them not merely as entertainment or cultural artifacts. No, narratives are indeed *más que cuentos*—beyond fantasy or story, or poetry or thick description, because they have the power to present reality and daily life, which for Latinx theology has always been a primary arena of God's salvific activity. God does not save exclusively or predominantly through extraordinary means, though certainly that is possible, but rather the Christian God is revealed in the quotidian, the everyday graced lives and experiences of Christians around the world.

As John O'Brien notes, narrative lies at the cornerstone of human self-understanding, of common experience, and therefore also of community and communal experience. Narrative therefore represents a natural methodological fit for the communion that is the church. By narrating the story of the church, rather than deducing its characteristics prescriptively from predetermined doctrines or abstract principles, we can build an ecclesiology that adequately represents the church: diverse and yet unified, like the body of Christ itself. The question before us, then, is how to integrate narrative into ecclesiology, and what sorts of narratives might prove most useful for this discipline. Latina theologian Michelle Gonzalez-Maldonado theorizes that literature can be used as source or resource for theology. I would expand on this claim, relating it specifically to the role of ecclesiology in narrating the story of the church. In that ecclesiological capacity, literature can be used as a resource in the sense of gathering data for the ecclesiological task. This is the sense in which literature serves as a listening device for the everyday lives of the faithful, and is particularly useful in discerning aspects of the *sensus fidei*. As a source of theology, literature can spark methodological insights, or deeper insights on God, understood as the Good, the True, the Beautiful, and the Just.

In this chapter, I examine whether and how art and literature serve the ecclesiological task as a resource by highlighting works from two Latinas: the Puerto Rican novelist and essayist Rosario Ferré, and a visual artist from the American Southwest, Yolanda López. This choice intends to lift up these women's work as exemplary and not exhaustive, as there is no doubt that religious understanding, especially regarding Catholicism and the role of the church in Latin American society and Latino culture more broadly, is ubiquitous in narratives emerging from what was once called the "New World."

Christianity, rooted in stories and narrative, constitutes a "people of the book" who worship the Word of God. Stories are embedded in our tradition. Dante and Milton, Dickens and Joyce, as well as Teresa of Avila, Juana Inés de la Cruz, and countless others, whether theologians or mystics, philosophers or writers, have woven a tapestry of stories that intertwine with the Christian story in myriad ways. Historian Sheridan Gilley writes that "the transition from the religion of the Word into other words has an importance which historians cannot neglect if they wish to understand Christian culture and its relationship to ecclesiastical history."[1] The same is true for ecclesiologists. Since the church is where culture and ecclesial history meet in dynamic fashion, ecclesiologists cannot afford to ignore the importance of story and narrative in the history, mission, and ministry of the church. The transition from Word to words includes biblical texts, but also encompasses a much broader range of narratives and other genres about Christianity, reacting to Christianity, and/or born of a Christian context. Certainly literary narratives, as well as other artistic expressions, are part of this list.

But the relationship between Christianity and literature has not always been a harmonious one. Literature has functioned to stoke anti-Catholicism as well as to nurture piety,

---

1. Sheridan Gilley, "Introduction," in *The Church and Literature,* Studies in Church History 48 (Rochester, NY: Boydell and Brewer, 2012).

and the church has encouraged the censorship of literature (one need think only of the longevity of the Index of Forbidden Books) at the same time as it nourished the arts with encouragement and patronage. Even the church's urge to forbid Catholics from having access to certain books attests to the power of literature to shape minds, define and redefine reality, including people's perception of faith. Thus the relationship between literature and Christian faith can be discerned even in the church's preoccupation with exposing Catholics to the right kind of stories, and protecting them from those that seemed dangerous or misleading. The worldviews of Catholics are informed by literature and a variety of aesthetic genres; these same genres reveal the intuitions of the faithful as well. As such, art forms and informs people's faith.

Faith-Filled Art, Artful Faith

One cannot overstate the power of art, including great literature, to encapsulate the human imagination and frame human reality. It does so in ways different from but no less revealing than history or the social sciences. David Tracy writes extensively about the power of the literary classic, with its superabundance of meaning, to convey truth—a notion he applies to scripture as a classic text.[2] In Tracy's reading, following Ricoeur, a richness of truth is to be found in the interaction between reader and text—a fusion of horizons that produces new understandings. Though literature serves neither as the exclusive or the most accessible artistic vehicle for aesthetic forms of truth telling, in the hispanophone world, a number of thinkers have highlighted the link between literature and theology. Latina theologian Michelle Gonzalez-Maldonado notes that theology and literature have historically been tied, citing the relationship between

---

2. See David Tracy, *The Analogical Imagination: Christian Theology and the Culture of Pluralism* (New York: Crossroad, 1998).

Gustavo Gutiérrez and the work of José María Argüedas as a prime example. Before her, Luis Rivera Pagán, Raúl Fournet-Betancourt, and other seminal theorists turned to literature as a guide in mapping the cultural imagination of the peoples of Latin America. In literary texts, these thinkers see reflected not only historical but attitudinal trends toward Christianity in general and Catholicism in particular. The church has historically been engrained in the social fabric of the lands colonized by Western European explorers, and the work of Latin American authors and chroniclers necessarily reflects these historical and attitudinal contours.

For Gonzalez, theologians can approach literature either as a theological resource or a theological source—a locus of theology.[3] To utilize literature as a resource for theology means to plumb literary texts for data about how theological themes are being understood in a particular context. Gonzalez refers to literature in this sense as a "vehicle for unearthing the intellectual heritage of Latin American peoples."[4] Peter Clarke's insight agrees with this sentiment. He notes that in the relationship between church and literature, one might explore either the representation of the church and its teachings in literature or the influence of different literary genres on Christian writing.[5] Historians have noted a range of themes (historical, philosophical, etc.) "that can be explored from literary material, including tensions between Christianity and culture."[6] Thus, theology benefits from exploring the way authors of literary works portray Christi-

---

3. Michelle Gonzalez, "Unearthing the Latino(a) Imagination: Literature and Theology, Some Methodological Gestures," in *New Horizons in Hispanic/Latino(a) Theology*, ed. Benjamin Valentín (Cleveland: Pilgrim Press, 2003), 119–37.

4. Here she is following the Puerto Rican theologian Luis Rivera-Pagán. See ibid., 122.

5. Peter Clarke, preface to *The Church and Literature* (Suffolk, UK: Boydell Press, 2012), ix.

6. Gilley, "Introduction," xix.

anity, the church, personal devotion, and spirituality, as well as understandings of God, salvation, sinfulness, and redemption in literature. Theologians can use this material to define or refine theological formulations, to understand how the church operates in a given socio-historical context, or to grasp how doctrines reflect the beliefs and practices of a group of people depicted in the form of a literary narrative. Narratives tell theologians how an author understands doctrinal formulations, sacramental operations, sacred doctrines, devotional practices. Literature thus serves as a resource for theology as a second-order discipline, which theorizes and systematizes people's reflections on experience. Though the vehicle is an artistic expression, theology nevertheless approaches the literary text as it would any data-mine.

Alternatively, according to Gonzalez, theologians might approach literature as a source for theology. She notes that "theology and literature share the ability to express the divine presence in people's daily lives."[7] Building on the aesthetic turn in theology exemplified in the work of Hans Urs von Balthasar and others, Gonzalez reminds readers that Christians have known God to be the Good, the True, and the Beautiful, and a key source of the beauty in literature lies in its capacity to portray reality. It is this insight that gives rise to the analysis in the next two chapters. If literature portrays reality through aesthetic means, it can serve as a source for theological reflection, particularly given the emphasis in Latino/a theologies on the graced status of ordinary daily life (or *lo cotidiano*, as many have called it). Thus, literary works can serve as resource and source, giving rise to new understandings of God, self, other, and community, and providing insights into the workings of the *sensus fidelium*. Further, as we will see in chapter 3, literature illuminates the complicated hermeneutical structures at work in the ecclesial use of power.

---

7. Gonzalez, "Unearthing the Latino(a) Imagination," 125.

This chapter examines two texts: a short story by Puerto Rican–born author Rosario Ferré, "The Battle of the Virgins," and the Guadalupe series of paintings by Chicana artist Yolanda López. The literary narratives and López's triptych are twentieth-century works with overlapping artist/ writers—Ferré was born in 1938 and López in 1942, while Daína Chaviano, the Cuban novelist whose work I will discuss in the next chapter, was born a generation later, in 1960. Each narrative exemplifies one approach to the role of literature in theology, and each is paired with insights from academic theologians that serve as fruitful conversation partners to the theological themes and challenges brought forth by the narratives. First, I will examine Ferré's story in the method of literature-as-theological-resource or data mine, particularly a resource for the interaction of popular Catholicism and the *sensus fidelium*. The innate sense of the faith that belongs to the whole people of God and, according to the Second Vatican Council is infallible, has long been a subject for U.S. Latino theologian Orlando Espín, who has written authoritatively on the subject of popular religion, popular Catholicism, and how these beliefs and practices relate to themes like the Tradition and the sense of the faithful (*sensus fidelium*). I will use Espín's insights to plumb the resources of Ferré's text in an effort to tease out the complexities of discerning the relationship between what the people of God believe and the infallible intuition of faith to which the council referred.

In the next chapter, I turn to Daína Chaviano's novel as a theological source, a locus of theological reflection on authority and space/place. There, the work of the late Ada María Isasi-Díaz proves a useful companion in explorations of how space, place, power, and authority interact, or could interact fruitfully in the church. Though different methodologies and different theological themes are in play in these chapters, both illuminate aspects of ecclesiology that are best investigated as an interplay between art and theory: the discernment of the *sensus fidei*, the hermeneutics of power in Roman Catholicism, and the importance of mapping *lo cotidiano* as we attempt to theologize the experience of the laity in a manner that will be useful for ecclesiology.

But first, a few caveats. This is by no means an exhaustive treatment of the intersection of literature and Christianity or Catholicism. I have selected literary pieces that appeal to me and have held meaning for me over time. Different theologians or thinkers might choose different narratives and arrive at divergent conclusions. I welcome this polyphony. For the most part, this text is based on investigations and themes that I find beneficial or interesting to the ecclesiological task. This foray is meant to be exemplary, an invitation to theologians to look seriously at literature as a vehicle for theological truth. As such, this effort is an initial step, and by no means a final pronouncement.

Ferré's "The Battle of the Virgins," Popular Catholicism, and the *Sensus Fidei*

One of the earliest insights Latinx theology brought to the mainstream theological community was the academic study of popular religiosity in its myriad forms. Indeed, to explore the ecclesiological intuitions of the Hispanic church, it has been necessary to examine those devotional, liturgical, home-based, and public acts that characterize the faith of these cultures. Pioneered by Orlando Espín, the study of popular Catholicism in particular serves as a cornerstone to any attempt at articulating an ecclesiology from a Latinx perspective, because popular Catholicism intersects with such key ecclesiological insights as Tradition, the sense of the faithful, and the self-understanding of the people of God. By no means does Espín's work, or that of anyone doing Latinx theology, claim or even imply that Latinos/as are the only cultural group with popular religious practices that should be studied, but his work focuses on that community. Because the focus on popular religiosity is essentially a spotlight on the religious practices of laypeople, Espín feels he addresses a major lacuna in contemporary ecclesiology, which he claims is "unsuccessful in theologizing on the laity."[8]

This lacuna may be attributed to the overemphasis in contemporary ecclesiology on magisterial documents (including the documents of Vatican II), so that academic theology dwells on doctrinal, text-based ecclesiology instead of coming forth from the pastoral source that should be its starting point. Espín's focus on the lived reality and lived religiosity of the laity offers a correction to this virtuosi-focused ecclesiology and makes important contributions to the reorientation of ecclesiology toward the whole people of God. It is my contention that there are many insights about the faith of the laity to be found in literary texts and, if theologians approach these texts as Gonzalez suggests in her "resource" category, we can discern the intuition of faith embedded there. By chronicling the lived reality of characters, literary narratives reveal religious understandings embedded in culture, language, and practices.

The brief personal essay "The Battle of the Virgins," by Puerto Rican author Rosario Ferré, is a prime example of text that can be used as a theological resource. Ferré's essay foregrounds the tension Espín describes between religious elites and the faith of the people and reveals a complex faith that is rooted in traditional devotional practices and prayer and subversive of a repressive patriarchal system this faith-tradition seems to endorse.

> No sooner has she begun to pray when I asked, "Why is *la Guadalupe* black? All the other Virgins I know are white and blond, and they have blue eyes."
>
> "She's not black, she's brown. She was buried in the ground for eight hundred years. The dirt stuck to her and now she's the same color as the earth."

---

8. Espín, *The Faith of the People*, 4.

"Why was she buried in the ground for eight hundred years?" I whispered.

"Because some bad men wanted to harm her. I saw the story in Tizoc, a Mexican movie I went to. Pedro Infante tells how la Guadalupe was hidden away in a cave in the mountains because they wanted to destroy her image. It was such a beautiful movie! Every time María Félix appeared on the screen, Pedro Infante and his mariachis played the guitar for her just like Eusebio does for me in El Tibidabo once in a while."[9]

This scene represents the first catechetical moment between the narrator of Ferré's short story (likely Ferré herself) and Gilda Ventura, the nanny in the story.[10] It also crystallizes the problematic nature of getting at the *sensus fidelium* by looking at popular religious practices and beliefs; namely, that these beliefs tend to be extradoctrinal or non-doctrinal, informed as much by popular belief and customs (and in this case, movies and popular culture) as they are by Vatican-approved Catholic teaching. This does not render the practices and beliefs irrelevant, however. In fact, the opposite holds true: I believe this scene represents the way in which divergent strands of knowledge and complex systems of sense making coalesce into a fundamental understanding of divine activity in the world that coincides with both the central teachings of Christianity and the faith of Christians themselves.

When the narrator joins Gilda at the cathedral in Ponce, praying before la Guadalupe, she is engaged in a traditional

9. Rosario Ferré, "The Battle of the Virgins," in *Goddess of the Americas: Writings on the Virgin of Guadalupe*, ed. Ana Castillo (New York: Riverhead Books, 1996), 81.

10. The story is told in the first person, so while it is safe to assume, given the similarities with Ferré's life, that the author is the narrator, I will nevertheless refer to the protagonist as "the narrator" because a name is not given.

religious practice. Outwardly, it would appear that two women kneeling in prayer in front of a Guadalupan statue is nothing out of the ordinary. Gilda's gloss on the virgin's story is somewhat noncanonical. Her version conflates the stories of Guadalupe de Extremadura with that of the Mexican virgin told in the accepted narrative, the *Nican Mopohua*. Gilda's version also includes strands from a cinematic treatment of the Guadalupan story that itself combines Mexican actors in retelling the story of a Spanish virgin. Nevertheless, it is this extranormative narrative that subverts the traditionally pious message and replaces it, or at least nuances it, with an understanding different from traditional Mariologies. "La Guadalupe is a very powerful virgin! You don't want her as your enemy. Those swords are her thunderbolts. She's not a namby-pamby virgin like the ones in the other churches. She gets things done and she protects people who fight for what they want."[11] Here, Gilda has picked up on the narrator's "misreading" of the rays of sunshine surrounding Guadalupe as samurai swords and uses this misreading to emphasize the power of the Virgin.

Unlike the "other" virgins, like the Immaculate Conception revered by the religious elites (personified in the narrator's mother and the rest of the high society in Ponce, as well as the bishop), Guadalupe is not passive, longsuffering, placidly standing on a bed of lilies. Guadalupe represents, for Gilda and for her charge, a powerful woman who protects those who follow their passions. This was indeed a subversive message for the young female narrator to hear, and for Gilda to proclaim. Both the narrator and Gilda were expected to conform to the socio-cultural expectations of their respective classes. For the narrator, this meant aspiring not to an education but to a placid family life where, by denying herself pleasure (particularly sexual pleasure) she would guarantee her soul's entrance into heaven. For Gilda,

---

11. Ferré, "Battle of the Virgins," 82.

the expectations were far more extreme: her family's poverty made it nearly impossible to fathom an education or any sort of liberation from the life of poverty to which she was surely doomed. And yet, at the end of the story neither woman has conformed to the Marianista[12] norms expected of them. Gilda improbably was able to leave the island and complete an education, becoming a nurse, and the narrator gains the courage to leave the island for boarding school and college in the United States.

Ferré's story ends with a shocking observation on the part of the now-adult narrator: "Gilda's life had been heroic; she was a fit example of a devotee of the Virgin of the conquistadors."[13] While the majority of Latin America (and other colonized cultures) might disagree with the characterization of conquistadors as heroic, I'd like to focus here on the juxtaposition of Gilda, a victim of the double rejection of being a woman and a Latina of the lower class in Puerto Rico and the mainland United States, with the heroic virtue of Guadalupe as understood by Gilda and the narrator: a powerful Virgin who protects those who fight for what they want. What Gilda wanted for herself and for her young charge was to break away from the expected feminine roles and into a life of their own, a life marked by love, passion, and education. Both Gilda and the narrator find this by leaving their homeland and seeking out something new. In rooting their liberative praxis in devotion to the Guadalupe in Ponce's cathedral, Ferré ties popular Catholic practice to goals that would be characterized as feminist: the self-actualization of women, their education, and their capacity for self-determination. This stands in stark contrast

---

12. The term "Marianismo" here is taken from Evelyn Steven's groundbreaking 1973 essay, "*Marianismo*: The Other Face of *Machismo* in Latin America," in *Female and Male in Latin America*, ed. A. Decastello (Pittsburgh: University of Pittsburgh Press, 1973).

13. Ferré, "Battle of the Virgins," 87.

to the magisterial teaching personified in the Irish-American Bishop MacManus, whereby women were expected to devote their lives to the avoidance of passion, shunning higher education in favor of having a respectable family. Late in the story, when Gilda asks the narrator what Marshmellow (the town's "Spanglish" nickname for Bishop MacManus) discussed at Mass, the young girl answers:

> "He said young women must pray so that when we get married our husbands will respect us during the act of procreation. He said decent men only marry young virgins." Gilda made a funny noise and screwed up her face. "Does he mean they don't marry old ones? Poppycock! What did he say about women going to the university?" "Nothing. He said we had to be like la Inmaculada. . . ."[14]

Gilda's devotion to Guadalupe, on the other hand, inspires independent thinking, education, and fulfillment, desires shared by her charge as evidenced in the child's determination to study in the United States. Far from the life of purity and self-denial MacManus prescribes for women based on devotion to la Inmaculada, Gilda's Marian devotion moves her toward self-determination, not subservience, and even toward sexual embodiment, not abstinence or frigidity, the two options offered by the bishop's take on la Inmaculada. Similar dreams, of self-determination and bodily integrity for example, echo today in worldwide movements for women's liberation and self-actualization that can be broadly characterized as feminist. Can these feminist impulses be said to be part of the sense of the faithful? The question for ecclesiologists looking to narratives such as these as a resource is how to determine the relationship between the portrayals of popular Catholicism in literature and the Catholic understanding of the *sensus fidelium, sensus fidei,* and *consensus fidelium,*

---

14. Ibid., 86.

which is the agreement of the whole church in matters of faith. How does literature-as-theological-resource relate to theological categories, and what criteria can be applied to relate these seemingly disparate discourses in a fruitful way?

Orlando Espín has emphasized the importance of popular Catholicism as a source for theology, "a conveyor of its own form of Tradition"[15] that complements what ecclesiologists have previously recognized as Tradition, because it represents a manifestation of the *sensus fidelium*. He writes:

> I insist that the people's faith be taken seriously as a true *locus theologicus* and not solely or mainly as a pastoral, catechetical problem. . . . The vast majority of Catholics in the history of the universal Church have always been and still are the lay poor. Consequently, given that Catholic doctrine holds that the Church is the infallible witness to revelation, then this *must* mean that the lay poor (i.e., the immense majority of the Church throughout twenty centuries) *are too* infallible witnesses to revelation. However, the way these millions have understood, received, and expressed their faith is undeniably "popular Catholicism." . . . Popular Catholicism is the real faith of the real Church.[16]

In studying the devotional practices, public acts, and home rituals of Catholics, theologians examine how the Tradition of the church has been received and interpreted by the people of God, and how this understanding is made manifest outwardly. The faith lives of the people of God serves as the source and the norm of how Tradition continues to be interpreted and how the gospel is continually revivified in the contemporary context. In short, it narrates the church's story—a central ecclesiological task. Literary texts should be treated

---

15. Orlando O. Espín and Sixto Garcia, "Sources of Hispanic Theology," *CTSA Proceedings* 43 (1988): 123.

16. Espín, *Faith of the People*, 3.

as an avenue for the discovery of these devotional practices, acts, and rituals as they function in the daily lives of communities. Frequently, these practices, such as home altars, prayer to specific saints, etc., appear in literary texts almost in the background as part of the setting. At times, as in the Ferré story, devotional practices like Marian prayer move the plot of the story along. No matter how popular Catholicism is featured by an author, though, the texts reveal much about the ways in which Catholic faith is made manifest in culturally specific ways and therefore should not be ignored.

Espín notes that a full and proper understanding of Tradition necessitates a richer understanding of the *sensus fidelium*, the sense of the faithful, or "intuitive grasp on the truth of God that is possessed by the Church as a whole, as a consensus."[17] Here Espín builds on the work of the major ecclesiologist of Vatican II, the Dominican Yves Congar. In particular, Espín draws on Congar's elaboration of the difference between Tradition and traditions, as well as the Second Vatican Council's understanding of the relationship between scripture and Tradition.[18] What Espín adds to the notion of Tradition is the narrative aspect of popular religiosity. Like many theologians, Espín understands one aspect of Tradition to be represented in the decrees of the ecumenical councils, interpreted in the writings of the fathers of the church, and communicated and witnessed by the magisterium of

---

17. Roger Haight, "Sensus fidelium," in *The HarperCollins Encyclopedia of Catholicism*, ed. Richard P. McBrien (San Francisco: HarperSanFrancisco, 1995), 1182.

18. Yves Congar, *Tradition and Traditions: the Biblical, Historical, and Theological Evidence for Catholic Teaching on Tradition* (Irving, TX: Basilica Press, reprint ed. 1997). Also Vatican II, *Dei verbum* (*Dogmatic Constitution on Divine Revelation*), 10. On the sources of Espín's notion of Tradition, see also J. Geiselmann, *The Meaning of Tradition* (New York: Herder & Herder, 1966); R. P. C. Hanson, *Tradition in the Early Church* (London: SCM Press, 1962); J. Walgrave, *Unfolding Revelation* (Philadelphia: Westminster Press, 1972).

theologians.[19] This dimension of Tradition is what most theologians understand by the term. However, Espín's notion of Tradition is expanded to include the living witness of the faithful throughout history, as embodied in the practices, beliefs, and devotions held by the majority of the people of God and reflected in their public prayer, their worship, and their artistic expression, including and especially literary expressions.

We should note that Espín does not equate popular Catholicism with the *sensus fidelium*. Rather, he avers that popular Catholicism is a manifestation of that "faith-full"[20] intuition of the people of God. "It is important to remember that what is the infallible bearer of revelation is the discerned, intuitive sense of the faith and not the many symbolic and historical ways employed as its inculturated expressions."[21] As a

---

19. Espín, *Faith of the People*, 65.

20. A helpful play on words used by Espín to denote the power of the people's faith present, indeed filling, their popular practices. Ibid., 63.

21. Ibid., 71. One should also bear in mind the distinction, made at Vatican II, between the *sensus fidei*, and the *sensus fidelium*. The *sensus fidei*, or sense of faith, refers to the intelligibility of the content of faith, the knowability of God by the faithful; the bishops at Vatican II refer to it as "the supernatural appreciation of the faith" (*Lumen gentium* 12). The *sensus fidelium*, or sense of the faith, is the sense of the community of the faithful, which "cannot err in matters of belief" (*Lumen gentium* 12). Some, like Herbert Vorgrimler, use the terms *sensus fidelium* and *consensus fidelium* interchangeably, but clearly Espín does not. See Herbert Vorgrimler, "From *Sensus Fidei* to "*Consensus Fidelium*," *The Teaching Authority of the Believers*, Concilium 180, ed. J. B. Metz and E. Schillebeeckx (Edinburgh: T&T Clark, 1985), 3–11. Perhaps the most helpful definition of the *sensus fidei/fidelium* distinction is from the International Theological Commission's "*Sensus Fidei* in the Life of the Church," which distinguishes between the *sensus fidei fidelis*, the supernatural instinct of believers as individuals to discern the truth of faith, and the *sensus fidei fidelium*, the church's communal instinct of faith by which the church recognizes and proclaims Christ. See "*Sensus Fidei* in the Life of the Church" at http://www.vatican.va, n. 4.

manifestation, it must be subject to interpretation, much like any attempt to articulate an intuition. "The main problem with the study of the *sensus fidelium* as a necessary component in any adequate reflection on Tradition is . . . its being a sense, an intuition. This sense is never discovered in some kind of pure state. . . . It is always expressed through the symbols, language, and culture of the faithful and therefore is in need of . . . interpretive processes and methods similar to those called for by the written texts of Tradition and scripture."[22] These interpretive processes begin in theological attempts at narrating the content, contexts, and significance of popular religious practices. In this way, the symbolic or aesthetic expressions of the *sensus fidelium* that make up popular religion must be subject to criteria of adequacy, in order to judge how congruent these expressions are with the whole of the Christian tradition.

The process of bringing the (necessarily pluralistic, divergent, multidisciplinary) narratives into dialogue with criteria of adequacy begins the conversation among the people of God, the academic theological community, and the magisterial documents, but in a way that is genuinely open to a shift in horizons of understanding.[23] Genuine dialogue, though potentially disruptive and dangerous, can and should be transformative as well. "If a sense of the faith is to be discerned as a true or false bearer of the Tradition, it must be capable of promoting the results expected of the Christian message and of Christian living."[24] The insights of popular Catholicism do not hold true, then, if their fruits are not borne out in lived commitment to Christian discipleship. In terms of Ferré's characters, Gilda's escape from a life of pov-

---

22. Espín, *Faith of the People*, 66.
23. See *Dei Verbum* 8: "This tradition which comes from the Apostles develops in the Church with the help of the Holy Spirit. For there is a growth in the understanding of the realities and the words which have been handed down."
24. Espín, *Faith of the People*, 67.

erty to one of self-determination and self-actualization, to my mind, meets these criteria.

Here it is helpful to recall the distinction mentioned at Vatican II between the *sensus fidelium* and the *sensus fidei*. Francis Sullivan distinguishes between the *sensus fidei* as a subjective sense and the "objective meaning" of the *sensus fidelium*, which refers to the content of the belief held by the faithful.[25] More helpful, though, is the 2014 document of the International Theological Commission, which eschews Sullivan's subjective/objective distinction in favor of a distinction based on the subject of the intuition of faith. So, for the ITC, the *sensus fidei fidelis* refers to the "personal capacity of the believer, within the communion of the church, to discern the truth of faith," whereas the *sensus fidei fidelium* refers not to the capacity of the individual but of the whole church. The *sensus fidei fidelium*, then, is the church's own instinct of faith by which she recognizes her Lord and proclaims his word."[26] The bishops of Vatican II, along with the ITC in using the term *sensus fidei*, are focused on the ability of the faithful to recognize the gospel by "connaturality."[27] Espín identifies popular religiosity as an outlet for the *sensus fidelium* but, because of the diversity of these often culturally conditioned

---

25. Francis A. Sullivan, *Magisterium: Teaching Authority in the Catholic Church* (New York: Paulist Press, 1983), 21–23.

26. ITC, *"Sensus Fidelium* in the Life of the Church," 4.

27. "Connaturality" is a Thomistic term. For a fuller treatment of these terms and how they are distinguished, see Richard Gaillardetz, *Teaching with Authority: A Theology of the Magisterium in the Church* (Collegeville, MN: Liturgical Press, 1997), esp. 121–32. See also ITC, "*Sensus Fidei* in the Life of the Church" 50: "The *sensus fidei fidelis* arises, first and foremost, from the connaturality that the virtue of faith establishes between the believing subject and the authentic object of faith, namely the truth of God revealed in Christ Jesus. Generally speaking, connaturality refers to a situation in which an entity A has a relationship with another entity B so intimate that A shares in the natural dispositions of B as if they were its own. Connaturality permits a particular and profound form of knowledge."

practices, it is important not to equate the *sensus fidelium* with the *consensus fidelium*, which is the universal agreement of the whole church on certain matters of faith. The liberative message of feminism or female self-actualization may be part of the *sensus fidei*, though it can certainly not be said to form part of the *consensus fidelium*. Instead, by indicating that popular religious practices express the *sensus fidei*, Espín implies that the insights or sense of faith expressed in these practices may differ among cultures with different customs.

The ITC agrees, devoting six paragraphs in its document to the relationship between popular religiosity and the *sensus fidei*.[28] However, the widespread nature of these practices in a variety of cultures, not all of them Hispanic, highlights the capability and willingness of a wide swath of the laity to engage their faith publicly. As the ITC notes, "popular religion springs from and makes manifest the *sensus fidei* and is to be respected and fostered."[29] It is those stories of popular religiosity that need telling and need to be incorporated more fully into the church's "official" doctrinal story and which should therefore feature prominently in contemporary ecclesiology.

The process of discerning the authenticity of the expression of popular Catholicism involves, according to Espín, three confrontations: With scripture, with the written texts of the Christian tradition, and with "the historical and sociological contexts in which the faithful intuitions and their means of expression occur."[30] Thus, popular religion does not become a *norma non normata*; it too must cohere with and be regulated by the whole of Tradition, even as it enriches that very Tradition.[31] At Vatican II, the bishops affirmed that

---

28. ITC, "*Sensus Fidei* in the Life of the Church," 107–12.
29. Ibid., 110.
30. Espín, *Faith of the People*, 66.
31. The bishops at Vatican II expressed the relatedness of Tradition in this way: "Sacred Tradition and sacred Scripture make up a single sacred deposit of the Word of God, which is entrusted to the Church" (*Dei verbum* 10).

the role of regulating, interpreting, and communicating the Church's Tradition was proper to the magisterium.[32] However, Espín stresses that the magisterium, though responsible for interpreting and communicating the church's Tradition, cannot be the sole arbiter of Tradition. He writes, "obviously, to claim that only the theologians or the bishops really understand revelation and, as a consequence, that only they should speak and express the faith in order to avoid deviations and error is to dismiss the *sensus fidelium* outright. . . ."[33] Here again, Espín's unwillingness to surrender interpretation to cultural or religious elites comes through. He clearly wants to create space for a genuine *sensus fidelium* that is both authoritative and egalitarian.

Thus, literature-as-theological-resource helps to broaden the chorus of voices contributing to the picture of what popular religious practices actually take place in communities, and to offer some insights as to the understandings behind these practices. Like Gilda's catechesis of her young charge in Ferré's narrative, the popular Catholic practices might reveal subversive understandings, and every effort should be made to place these understandings in dialogue with the messages being promulgated by the dominant culture and the religious elites in charge of making meaning. Hermeneutically, the task is monumental. However, it is only when this

---

32. *Dei verbum* continues: "But the task of giving an authentic interpretation of the Word of God, whether in its written form or in the form of Tradition, has been entrusted to the living teaching office of the Church alone. . . . Yet this magisterium is not superior to the Word of God, but is its servant. It teaches only what has been handed on to it. At the divine command and with the help of the Holy Spirit, it listens to this devotedly, guards it with dedication and expounds it faithfully. All that it proposes for belief as being divinely revealed is drawn from this single deposit of faith. It is clear, therefore, that, in the supremely wise arrangement of God, sacred Tradition, sacred Scripture and the Magisterium of the Church are so connected and associated that one of them cannot stand without the others" (10).

33. Espín, *Faith of the People*, 81.

harmony is brought about that we will truly be theologizing from the faith of the people.

The Literary-Artistic-Theological Connection: Yolanda López's Guadalupe Triptych

Narratives can be written or literary, but they certainly do not have to be. Similarly, nonwritten or literary artifacts can be read as texts. Like literature, visual art can function as a text: rife with symbolism and meaning, it can be a way of communicating with an audience without words. Theological aesthetics, a field increasingly engaged by Latino/a theologians, examines art and beauty as a symbol for God and locus of revelation. As Cecilia González-Andrieu writes, "Art, the work of human persons to reveal beauty, is patterned on the work of God. In mediating beauty, art is a channel which carries forward the purpose of the Cross."[34] Similarly, art can carry, embedded within it, a reflection of the *sensus fidelium*, in much the same way as literature does. By reflecting the artist's understanding of faith, even new or subversive understandings as the one in Ferré's story above, art mediates God's presence in the community of faith.

Yolanda López, a California-based, Chicana feminist artist, is of a similar generation as Rosario Ferré. The latter was born in 1938 and López in 1942. Though both women are obviously Latina, their cultural contexts could not be more different. López was reared in a working-class family, a multigenerational household that included her Mexican immigrant grandparents. Her mother, Margaret Singer, worked outside the home. Yolanda and her siblings grew up with her extended family. It was not until she attended col-

---

34. C. González-Andrieu, "How Does Beauty Save? Evocations from Federico García Lorca's Teoría Y Juego del Duende," *Cithara* 51, no. 1 (2011): 5–21, 68.

lege that López became interested in the Chicano/a movement that was underway in California. López, electrified by the consciousness raising, soon became an activist, working in San Diego and Southern California. At the same time, she was developing her artistic talent and donating her work to Chicano/a publications. Eventually she earned an MFA from the University of California at San Diego. Her most famous work, a triptych entitled "Our Lady of Guadalupe," depicts three generations of women in her family reimagined as the revered patroness of Mexico: her grandmother, her mother, and a self-portrait of the artist herself.

The triptych, done in oil pastels, imagines three ordinary women as the extraordinary virgin revered in Mexico and across the Americas—the very virgin revered by Gilda in Ferre's story. To reinterpret such an iconic symbol is a subversive act, and when López's images first emerged (in 1978), many were outraged, staging protests and threatening the Mexican magazine that had published them.[35] Knowing she had hit a nerve, López was pleased, saying, "People either really were excited and loved it or were disturbed by it. . . . That's when I knew I was on to something. It hit the twitch meter."[36] The images are breathtaking in their ordinariness: one depicts an old woman sitting, holding a knife and a snakeskin. Another shows a middle-aged woman hunched over a Singer sewing machine, looking up from behind eyeglasses. The third shows the artist as a young woman, jogging, with the Guadalupan cape of stars casually thrown over a shoulder. All three share the Guadalupan halo of sunbeams (which, as mentioned earlier, Ferre's literary character interpreted as samurai swords), and other motifs such as a snake and an angel whose wings are the colors of the Mexican flag.

---

35. Lili Wright, "Yolanda López's Art Hits 'Twitch Meter' to Fight Stereotypes," *Salt Lake Tribune,* May 14, 1995, E. 3.

36. Ibid.

López is clearly experimenting with national symbolism and sacred imagery, integrating this sacred into the ordinary images of women she knows best: her mother, grandmother, and herself. In doing this, the artist replicates a central theme echoed by Latinx theologians: the holiness of *lo cotidiano*, or the everyday. In a piece on López's work from 1995, Lili Wright of the *Salt Lake Tribune* writes:

> Instead of depicting the virgin in traditional passive pose—hands crossed, eyes dreamy—López places three mortal woman within the virgin's sun-ray halo: herself, her mother and grandmother. All three women are seen as active, capable and engaged. López jogs. Her mother runs a sewing machine. And her grandmother skins a snake.
>
> It was López's way of providing role models, while paying homage to working-class women. "To pay honor to the ordinary, that's what interests me," she says. "I am not as interested in the extraordinary."[37]

The article contains several significant insights. Wright notices the difference between the active, engaged women of López's work and the traditionally passive posture of traditional Guadalupan imagery ("eyes dreamy"). This contrast, much like the contrast between the Immaculate Conception and Guadalupe in Ferre's story, hints at a bifurcation, or at least a plurality, of understandings of what makes women's religious role models sacred or holy. Is it passivity and long-suffering that women are to emulate in Mary? Or is there an undercurrent of revolt against these constraining images of silence disguised as holiness that López and Ferré are touching on? López wishes to "honor the ordinary," *lo cotidiano*, a theme Latinx theology has lifted up as a locus of revelation. Ferré, López, and Latinx theologians overlap in their desire

---

37. Ibid.

to lift up, honor, even make sacred the unacknowledged parts of life—the private sphere, the overlooked everyday that is the site of struggle for so many Latinos and Latinas in particular.

The mundane nature of the women's appearance and postures—working, sitting, jogging—juxtaposed with the otherworldly elements of Guadalupan imagery blend together in homage to the lives of Latinas, whose struggle has kept their families and, to a large extent, the church afloat. But there is a certain mundane quality to the image of Guadalupe herself, ubiquitous in Mexican and Mexican-American iconography, present in nearly every context from bodegas to laundromats to telenovelas. Described by Gloria Anzaldúa as "the single most potent religious, political, and cultural image of the Chicano/mexicano,"[38] this Marian image is everywhere. As historian Karen Mary Davalos notes in her excellent overview of López's work,

> when López began the investigation that resulted in [the Guadalupe series], the Virgin was appearing on murals and storefronts, on banners at rallies and demonstrations and even on cars as hood ornaments and exterior detailing. She was also vital in private domains, holding a central place in home altars, and in body adornment, tattooed on back and arms and engraved on religious medallions.[39]

The image of Guadalupe was an image of the supernatural woven throughout the everyday.

In a sense, then, the images in López's triptych combine two everyday Chicana images—working women and

38. Gloria Anzaldúa, *Borderlands/La Frontera: The New Mestiza* (San Francisco: Aunt Lute, 1987), 30.

39. Karen Mary Davalos, *Yolanda M. López* (Los Angeles: UCLA Chicano Studies Research Center Press, 2008), 80.

Guadalupe—and in the process subvert both. The tradi-tional image of Guadalupe's passivity and her presumed silence and long-suffering were subverted in López's depic-tions of Guadalupe as active, strong, working, and running. Similarly, the stereotypical image of Mexican and Mexican-American women, as either oversexualized bombshells or mournful abuelitas, was replaced with images of ordinary women taking their place in the public sphere through labor that created hope. López herself claimed that in particular she wanted the "Mother" image—the depiction of her mother sewing the gold stars onto the Guadalupan cape—to be a "homage to all working mothers," saying, "living breathing women also deserve the respect and love lavished on Gua-dalupe. It is a call to look at women, hardworking enduring and mundane, and the heroines of daily life."[40]

This migration from idealized passivity to ordinary engagement mirrors the methodological move necessary in ecclesiology. Just as the ubiquitous depictions of Guada-lupe rarely incorporated the lived reality of Chicanas in the late twentieth century, so too an ecclesiology that proceeds deductively from abstract principles fails to address the real life of the church as it is experienced by believers. Art, whether literary or studio art, can build a bridge between *lo cotidiano* and the Beautiful, and theorists such as ecclesiolo-gists would do well to position ourselves on that bridge.

López did not set out to create explicitly religious art. In fact, according to Davalos, she left the church as a young woman, after a priest declined to give last rites to López's dying cousin. Rather than invalidate López's insights about Guadalupan imagery, the ecclesial violence that drives her away from Catholicism lends this art a particular poignancy. For Chicanas and other Latinas throughout the United States and Latin America, Guadalupe is an inescapable image, an

---

40. Betty LaDuke, "Yolanda López: Breaking Chicana Stereo-types," *Feminist Studies* 20, no. 1 (1994): 121.

ideal one cannot ignore. Catholicism functions in much the same way—ubiquitous in Latin America and in Latinx cultures in art and architecture, in language, and in symbols that permeate high and low culture.

But as inspiring as the story of Guadalupe can be, and as widespread as the devotion to Guadalupe is, her image is not unproblematic. For López, the overwhelming cloak in the traditional Guadalupan imagery serves as a symbol of constraint, preventing the virgin from moving freely, exposing only her face and hands.[41] In depicting Guadalupe in shorts, or a housedress, or a working woman's clothing, López celebrates movement, liberates Guadalupe from her constricting cloak, even in the self-portrait slinging it over her shoulder like an accessory rather than a burden. Furthermore, López replaces the downward glance of the traditional Guadalupan images with women who look straight out at the viewer. The grandmother figure is seated and looking straight ahead with a tired but serene expression. The Margaret Singer-as-Guadalupe figure looks up from her sewing machine, over her glasses and at the viewer as well. The self-portrait of López as Guadalupe is even more dynamic, appearing to run at the person looking at the art. Moreover, by refusing to settle on just one image of Guadalupe and opting for a multiplicity of women that incorporate generations and states of life, López moves away from idealized notions of womanhood to celebrate and "validate working-class women's experiences."[42] This move away from idealized notions and toward the reality of human life echoes the move in theology, especially since the Second Vatican Council, to move away from static notions of perfection in the church and toward a more complex portrait that adequately accounts for the church's participation in the world.

---

41. Karen Mary Davalos, *Yolanda M. López,* 88.
42. Ibid., 87.

Women's Art and the Sense of Faith

This notion of women as the heroines of their lives and their communities, precisely in their ordinary, hardworking endurance, belongs to the sense of faith of the Latino/a community and contributes a much-needed refocusing to the church's views of holiness, of the laity, and of women in particular. López's art and Ferré's story belong to that aspect of tradition highlighted by Espín: popular Catholicism. The women's work reflects faithful intuitions about God, specifically about women as *imago Dei,* in their depictions of women as architects of their own destinies, freed from patriarchal control.

Ferré and López refocus our sense of holiness by lifting up *lo cotidiano,* the everyday, as a locus of revelation that is as important (and more ubiquitous) than the extraordinary holiness most Catholics understand as the norm. Rather than heroic acts of extraordinary valor or faithfulness under torture that characterize hagiographies and stories of holiness, in focusing on the everyday lives of women, these artists chart a different path to the sacred, a more ordinary, but more broadly available way. These artists also challenge the idea of a holiness that requires a rejection of the material world in favor of the divine, as if the divine did not participate in materiality. Rather than lift up a cloistered life of prayer and mystical reflection, both Ferré's and López's Guadalupan images depict women's lives in their messiness: in relationship, at work, subject to poverty. One of López's collage pieces, *Madre Mestiza,* which she used as a study for the Guadalupe triptych, depicts a nursing mother in indigenous dress, wearing a *huipil,* a traditional loose, embroidered dress commonly worn in Mexico and other parts of Central and South America.[43] The similarities with Guadalupe are obvious, as López chooses an indigenous woman to

---

43. Ibid., 83.

put in Guadalupe's place, surrounding her with the rays of light from the original image. But the bodiliness of López's *Madre Mestiza* cannot be denied—her nurturing of a child is physical and embodied, not merely spiritual or mystical. Similarly, Gilda's catechetics on Guadalupe as a "virgin who protects those who fight for what they want" grounds Guadalupan devotion, in contrast to the otherworldly focus of the elite's devotion to the Inmaculada. In making Gilda, the joyful, beautiful, makeup-wearing, boyfriend-loving, young vibrant woman a devotee of Guadalupe, and then writing Gilda's success into the end of the story, Ferré pushes the boundaries of what holiness looks like for Latinas. Specifically, she broadens the notion of what Marian devotion looks like: not silent, passive, quiet women praying for departed souls alone, but vibrant active women, poor women, women who express their sexuality in relationships: they, too, are devoted to Guadalupe, and they, too, deserve a place at the table of models of holiness.

When one reads in *Lumen Gentium* that through the faithful intuition of the *sensus fidei*, "the people of God adheres unwaveringly to the faith given once for all to the saints, penetrates it more deeply with right thinking, and applies it more fully in its life,"[44] it is clear to see the function of women's artistic production in bringing this to fruition. López and Ferré penetrate more deeply into the idea of what holiness means and broaden this idea based on the lived reality of Latinas in the Caribbean and the American West. Two elements are interesting in these women's reinterpretation of holiness. First and most surprisingly is the similarity between these two portraits of Guadalupe—Ferré's literary depiction of a warrior virgin who protects those engaged in the daily struggle for life and, in particular, the self-portrait of López as Guadalupe running, self-possessed, active, and engaged. The two artists, while generational contemporaries,

---

44. *Lumen Gentium* 12.

approach Guadalupan devotion from different contexts. Ferré was a wealthy woman living in the Caribbean, while López is a woman who grew up in a working-class family in California. That these two women have such similar insight about Guadalupe as an incarnate force for woman's self-actualization points not necessarily to some supernatural intervention but instead to how widespread this view of Marian devotion might be, or how intense the hunger for alternate images of Guadalupe actually is. Women subverting what is viewed as holy in received images of Mary or any other saint must also be part of what we understand as the *sensus fidei*, not merely what coincides exactly with previous understandings of femininity or holiness. Otherwise, the *sensus fidei* would function only as a seal of approval on received wisdom, not as a source of wisdom in its own right. Its function would remain in the realm of ratification of top–down ideas about God, whereas the work of these women shows the *sensus fidei* to be a fundamentally creative function in the church.

A second surprising element of Ferré's and López's work lies in the sanctification of the nonwhite, nonwealthy, nonmale body. In this way, the image of holiness lifted up in these works is decidedly marginal. Gilda and the images of the Guadalupe triptych represent what theorists have called the double marginalization of Latinas through sexism and racism. The character of Gilda adds classism to this list as well, as Ferré portrays Gilda to be a victim of the narrator's mother's racial and socio-economic prejudices. Sadly, the canon of saints does not reflect the face of the majority of the people of God, the lay poor as Espín points out. Too often, these holy lives come and go in obscurity, without postulators in Rome to take up the cause of their canonization. Instead, it is up to artists and writers to lift up these holy lives lived in everyday struggle. While we know that the whole people of God shares in Christ's ministry of priest, prophet, and king, too often Christians forget that this necessarily includes the marginalized, the poor, people of color, and women. Art such as López's reminds everyone, not just Latinos/as, of the radical holiness embedded in these communities.

Along with reimagining what we mean by holiness, these artists' work reminds us of the call in *Lumen Gentium* for a partnership between the laity and the clergy in the task of evangelization.[45] Too often, the laity can be viewed as "junior associates" in the partnership between them and the clergy: expected merely to follow where the pastors lead, to offer only obedience and not initiative. In reimagining Guadalupe from women's perspectives, these artists stake out new territory in the devotional lives of Catholics, broadening our understanding of holiness and contributing novel images of a familiar icon. Any genuine partnership or dialogue between religious virtuosi, including clergy, and the laity, who are the majority of the people of God, cannot consist merely of the initiative of the virtuosi and the response of the laity. Instead, true dialogue and true partnership involve listening, as well as being able to surrender the initiative and to follow where the laity lead. Through their art, these women lead to the sanctification of ordinary life, to the uplifting of the female body in its diversity and complexity, to the mystery of the Incarnation of God in a marginalized body. Thus the roles of the clergy and the laity are reversed in these works. Gilda's clashes with McManus's notions of female holiness and passivity, as well as López's earthy images, help us to see that at times novel interpretations of holiness and sanctity come from the people, not merely from the hierarchical church. The laity must not merely follow, because the laity's experiences in the secular, embodied, and messy world lead to new and sometimes better understandings of proper prayer and worship. At times it is the laity who must lead and the clergy who must follow or listen. This lesson is

---

45. *Lumen Gentium* 33.

embedded in literature and art, and also in the doctrine of the *sensus fidelium* itself.

Within the partnership between the clergy and the laity, where the laity at times must take leadership in evangelization, the work of López and Ferré specifically signals the importance of women as creators of popular Catholicism, and not merely followers or custodians of an unchanging tradition. In fact, these women's reinterpretations of Guadalupan iconography (for López) and of Guadalupan devotion (in Ferré's case) remind us that tradition must be dynamic, because it is a living thing incarnate in communities. Rather than safeguarding a static model of the "deposit of faith," these women do what countless Christians have done before them—interpret the good news in light of their circumstances. For Ferré, this interpretation rejects predetermined roles for women in favor of self-determination, and Guadalupe serves as a champion for that vision. For López, Guadalupan iconography was insufficiently diverse and overly idealized even as it was omnipresent. Her reinterpretation incorporates the lived experience of the women she knew best in a celebration of women's survival and tenacity in difficult and demeaning circumstances. Both artists depict paths to holiness not traditionally emphasized for women. In this way, both contribute to notions of holiness; both open avenues into the self-understanding of the people of God. Both artists touch on the sense of faith of the church, especially the women in that church.

López and Ferré, who never met, who were separated geographically and culturally and who had differing experiences and affiliation with Roman Catholicism, depict a well-known, ubiquitous Marian image in subversive ways, as powerful active women who are at once holy and ordinary. This vision of holiness in the laity, especially in strong women, is part of the sense of faith, and this strain of holiness deserves attention. It is advisable for ecclesiologists to pay attention to art and literature as a resource, to see how

Christianity and Christian symbols, especially those ubiquitous ones we take most for granted, are depicted in the realm of aesthetics in order to overhear the faith-filled intuitions of the people of God.

Conclusion

The aesthetic turn in theology that was in vogue a decade or so ago, bolstered by interest in the work of Hans Urs von Balthasar, for example, can suffer from too strong a temptation of otherworldliness. Beauty becomes an element of a "God's-eye view" of reality, detached from the struggle and sinfulness, messiness and ambiguity of human life. Latinx theologians work against this view of aesthetics, positing instead that beauty and art serve to highlight the messiness of life and make it sacred—the holy in the midst of the ordinary. Both artists featured in this chapter embody this quotidian view of the sacred. Ferré's short story and López's Guadalupan triptych draw attention to a beautiful, if subversive, dimension of Guadalupan devotion. They do this in the midst of a fallen and finite world. Ferré's story, after all, only implicitly raises questions of race and class that affected the lives of the two central characters in the story. Ferré's own socioeconomic situation goes uninterrogated, and the complexity and violence of colonial reality in the Caribbean lie dormant, awaiting interpretation or explanation. López's complex relationship with Roman Catholicism colors her understanding of the work she does with Guadalupan imagery, but the results are no less subversively spiritual than Ferré's Gilda's understanding of the Mexican virgin. López's intergenerational, embodied depictions of Guadalupe remind the church of the messiness of the holiness the church proclaims.

What does this messiness and ambiguity, subversion and reinterpretation of imagery have to do with the task of ecclesiology? López and Ferré allow ecclesiologists a glimpse of the faith-filled intuitions of the people of God. The work of these artists serves as a repository of the *sensus fidelium*. Though the work of two women cannot be equated with the entirety of the faithful intuition of the people of God, when theologians attend to art and literature of a particular community, they overhear the intuitions that we call the sense of the faithful. These intuitions are embedded in artistic expression, and artistic expressions of this kind form and are formed by popular Catholicism. A central feature of Latinx Catholicism and a cornerstone of Latinx theology, popular religiosity, and specifically popular Catholicism, constitutes a unique contribution from the U.S. Latinx perspective to the global church. Not that popular religious practices are unique to the Latinx communities in the United States and abroad, as each ethnic and cultural group brings its own inculturated manifestation of Catholicism to bear on the universal church. However, Latinx theologians like Orlando Espín have pioneered the study of this phenomenon and made it matter in theology.

In the field of ecclesiology, popular Catholic belief and practice matter because they reflect the sense of the faithful. To the extent that art and literature highlight popular Catholicism and devotion, they contain embedded within them traces of that faithful intuition, which ecclesiologists can then tease out. This is vitally important work, as it grounds ecclesiology in the faith of the people of God, and at the same time challenges the church to broaden its notions of holiness, the role of the laity, and particularly the importance of women in the interpretation and transmission of the faith. The *sensus fidelium*, etched in the art and literature of a people, makes a contribution to ecclesiology "from below." In seeking to tell the story of the church, then, it behooves ecclesiologists to read the church's stories, take in the church's artistic production, inquire about the symbols and icons as created and interpreted by believers. But not only that, theologians must also pay attention to the aesthetic production of those on the margins of the church—whether pushed out, as

López was, by the disdain of a fellow Catholic, or alienated, as so many others are for whatever reason. Any reinterpretation of Catholic symbols can potentially convey something about the belief of the people. And, while not all these will be orthodox or necessarily expressed fully in one story or work, the theologian should nevertheless strive to listen to the faithful intuition about God embedded in the beauty a community can produce.

Art and literature provide a resource for theology, particularly as a record or trace of the sense of faith. But literature can function in another way as well, as a source for theology, not merely guiding content but indicating new methodological pathways. Using aesthetics as a starting point for discerning the sense of the faithful initiates a dialogue in the church between the laity and those religious elites who promulgate and officially interpret doctrine. Theologians stand at a hybrid point between these two constituencies—and literature as well as art can help navigate the complex hermeneutical terrain of dialogue. The next chapter takes up the task of examining how literature can function as theological source for ecclesial dialogue, particularly in a polarized church.

CHAPTER THREE

Dando lugar y haciendo espacio
Literature as Source
for Ecclesiology

How might the process of harmonizing the stories of the people of God with our theories about the ecclesial community take place? This question has particular resonance in an ecclesial climate marked by scandal and division, often characterized by mistrust between the bishops and the laity in the Catholic Church. To navigate this complex terrain, we turn to Michelle Gonzalez's second paradigm for integrating literature and theology: the use of literature as source. The following section will examine the novel *El hombre, la hembra, y el hambre* by Daína Chaviano, treating it as one would traditionally approach a theological text, by allowing it to spark insights in the reader about ecclesiology specifically. I examine the novel as an allegory for the people of God, including and especially the relationships between the magisterium, theologians, and the laity within that body. By juxtaposing the novel with the work of Ada María Isasi-Díaz, I show the methodological import of space and place in ecclesiology, not in a geographic or architectural sense, but in a hermeneutical one. Ecclesiology in the third millennium must be remapped with particular attention to the contributions of the laity, especially women. This demonstrates how literature can serve as more than a data mine for ecclesiology, though the function of literature as a way of overhearing the *sensus fidelium* is crucial. Literature as a theological source allows theologians the freedom to plumb not-explicitly-religious texts for new methodological, topical, or contextual realities.

Hombres, Hembras, y Hambres: Literature as Source for Ecclesial Hermeneutics

Esta isla se vende. Ni siquiera se subasta: se vende al por mayor. No sólo su mano de obra, sino también su alma; cada creencia, cada versículo, cada canto de sus religiones, cada pincelada de quienes la dibujaron durante siglos. Y ahí están esos que vienen con toda su cultura a cuestas, pero que siguen sin entender nada. . . . Tal vez de eso se trate: de creerse a toda costa lo que le pongan a uno delante, sin cuestionarse mucho. . . . ¿O estaré siendo injusta? Quizás sea muy difícil llegar al fondo de este enredo. Incluso para nosotros. No hay Dios ni cristiano que entienda que carajos pasa aquí. A lo mejor estamos tan aislados que nos hemos convertido en otra especie. Somos bichos raros. Los cubanos somos los marcianos de la Tierra, y sólo un extraterrestre puede entender lo que le pasa a otro.

—Claudia's first words in
El hombre, la hembra y el hambre.[1]

---

1. Daína Chaviano, *El hombre, la hembra y el hambre* (Barcelona: Planeta, 1998), 23. "This island is for sale. It's not even up for auction, it's wholesale. Not only its handiwork, but also its soul; every belief, every verse, every hymn of its religions, every brushstroke by all those who designed it through the centuries. And there are those who come with all their culture, but still understand nothing. . . . Maybe that is what it's about: believing at all costs whatever is put in front of you, without much questioning. . . . Or perhaps I'm being unfair? Maybe it's very difficult to get to the bottom of this mess. Even for us. There is neither God nor Christian who understands what the hell is going on here. Maybe we are so isolated that we have become another species. We're strange creatures. We Cubans are the Martians of the earth, and

The quotation above expresses much of what many Catholics have experienced in recent years regarding the church—a sense of loss, of being unmoored, of feeling incredibly isolated from and yet remaining committed to the Catholic communities that we inhabit. As a woman, a Catholic, and a scholar, particularly in interactions with students, I've felt a bit like the alien described above. Why do we stay? What is the pull of the Catholic Church? Whence this allegiance for an institution that can seem so broken at times?

A temptation of ecclesiology can be to remain in the idealistic realm, focusing on the principles that animate the church, the God that suffuses the church, the paschal mystery that gives rise to the church. This idealism seems to contradict many of the foundational principles of U.S. Latino/a theology, based in themes like the everyday, the popular, the grassroots, and the historically silenced communities from which many of us descend. And yet the historical moment that the church currently traverses seems ill fitted to idealism; instead it cries out for a touch of reality, of rootedness in experience, particularly in the unspoken or discounted experience of the silenced, the ignored, and the victims. There are, then, two questions that enliven my inquiry in this chapter: What should ecclesiology do in this historical moment marked by scandal, silence, and silencing? And where are the Latina/o ecclesiologists' voices in this?

My desire to name the present condition of the church, which survives and thrives in many places despite being mired in scandal and going bankrupt in ways that exceed the financial bankruptcies we hear about on the news, brought to mind the *período especial* in Cuba—an economic crisis precipitated by the collapse of the Soviet Union and the drying up of the financial support that it provided the Cuban government. These events brought about a period of intense lack

---

only one extraterrestrial can understand what another one is going through" (*my translation*).

on the island. This lack of resources spurred great suffering: hunger, corruption, and finally the *balsero* phenomenon of 1994, when severe poverty and desperation prompted nearly fifty thousand Cubans to take to the sea in makeshift rafts in an attempt to escape toward something better. Many died, some wound up in Guantanamo Bay, some successfully emigrated to the United States.[2] While there has been much academic work on the *período especial*,[3] and many creative projects as well (including a 2002 movie, *Balseros*), one particular literary portrait of that historical moment seemed most apt as a frame for the ecclesiological task: *El hombre, la hembra y el hambre*, a magical-realist novel by Daína Chaviano, a Cuban author who emigrated to the United States in 1991.

I do not intend to describe the ways in which the contemporary people of God struggle with the sex-abuse crisis (and other crises), the continuing disaffiliation trends (which will be discussed later in this book), or the various other crises that face Catholicism and the world today. Rather, my goal is to examine how literary texts, when undertaken as an exercise in narrating and dialoguing, and hermeneutical triangles of conversation—not unlike the triad of *hombre/hembra/hambre* in the novel—chart a path for ecclesiology and represent an avenue in which U.S. Latinx theologies lead the charge toward a renewed but undetermined future of Catholicism. I will begin by paralleling the triad in the title

---

2. See "The Cuban Rafter Phenomenon" at http://balseros.miami.edu.

3. Examples of this academic work include Ariana Hernandez-Reguant, ed., *Cuba in the Special Period: Culture and Ideology in the 1990s* (New York: Palgrave Macmillan, 2009); Julio Carranza Valdés and Juan Valdés Paz, "Institutional Development and Social Policy in Cuba: 'The Special Period,'" *Journal of International Affairs* 58, no. 1 (Fall 2004): 175–88; James K. Galbraith, Laura Spagnolo, and Daniel Munevar, "Inequidad salarial en Cuba durante el periodo especial," *América Latina Hoy* 48 (2008): 109–40; Luis Suárez Solazar, "Cuba: La politica exterior en el periodo especial," *Estudios Internacionales* 27, no. 107/108 (1994): 307–34.

of the book to an ecclesiological triad—a hermeneutical triangle that consists of the whole people of God, and the ecclesiological actors who have particular roles in terms of narrating the stories of the people of God, bishops and theologians. The chapter will then turn to the importance of narrative as a source for ecclesiology specifically, and to the special role that U.S. Latinx theologies play in that turn toward narrative and explorations of place and space, exemplified in the work of *mujerista* theologian Ada María Isasi-Díaz on Havana as a space/place of identity and mission, an example of the centrality of the pastoral viewpoint in Latinx theology. This chapter, then, is an exercise in literary-theological symbiosis. What we see and experience in reading illuminates and helps us make sense of our historical reality, including our ecclesial reality.

Chaviano's 1998 magical-realist novel, *El hombre, la hembra y el hambre,* narrates the fantastic and disturbing story of a woman with a bifurcated identity who travels through a troubled city (Havana, Cuba) experiencing either auditory hallucinations, delusions, or mystical experiences, depending on one's viewpoint. The protagonists, Claudia and "La Mora," are the same person—seemingly before and after desperation drove this woman to prostitute herself to provide for her child, but the identities also coexist in time. The title refers to a triad of a man, a woman, and hunger, and each part of this triad bleeds into the others. Identity, context, and reality are all fluid and multiple in the story. The narrative is set in the Havana of the 1990s, in the throes of the *período especial,* where Claudia, a woman with a college degree and a job, lives in a dark, sadly not-unthinkable world in which prostitution proves more prosperous than her work as an art historian.

Readers meet Claudia and her alter ego, "La Mora," through the eyes of two of her lovers, Rubén and Gilberto. Their apprehensions of the same woman vary so wildly that they do not suspect her to be the same person at any point save the end of the story; nor does Rubén realize that the child Claudia struggles to keep alive is his. The sexualized gazes of the men define some of the reader's earliest impressions of Claudia/La Mora, but they do not contain her. In fact, the reader discovers that there is little that can contain this character who moves in alternate worlds inhabiting a variety of identities. Rubén and Gilberto comprise the main *hombres* in the narrative, along with the otherworldly and silent "Indio," whose scarred body serves as a reminder of the island's violent colonial past and a harbinger of misfortune to Claudia specifically.

The *hembra* in the narrative triad is Claudia/La Mora, an educated woman who turns to prostitution in order to provide for her child. Claudia is a person of multiple personalities, but not in the pathological sense. Rather, she enjoys inhabiting different characters throughout her life.[4] As she wanders the streets of Havana looking for ways to make ends meet, she undergoes what theologians might see as profoundly mystical experiences—ecstatic, otherworldly moments where she is transported to a different time and place that is at once rooted in contemporary time and space and yet utterly unlike it, almost to the point of being unrecognizable. It is this context, itself fluid and ever changing, that marks the third part of the triptych in the title, and that serves as a significant character in its own right. The stories and histories of Havana and indeed of the entire island are revisited through Claudia's hallucinations/otherworldly experiences. The setting itself has multiple personalities, ranging from the post-Conquista pueblo to the era after independence to the pre-Castro city and the present city in the grips of the economic crisis. *El hambre*, or hunger, is the thread that unites these pluralistic settings, whether it is hunger for justice, for revenge, for sex, or for material or spiritual

---

4. See Maribel Tamargo, "Hipertexto, ciudad e historia en *El hombre, la hembra y el hambre: una reflexión*," *Confluencia* 24, no. 1 (2008): 181–86.

sustenance. The notion of hunger further provides a backdrop of urgency—exemplified when the narrator informs the reader at the outset of the novel that Claudia's life is about to change, and while she is aware of this, and despite her many moments of mystical ecstasy and the fortune-telling spirits that visit her, she does not yet know what the radically different future will look like.

This work of magical realism by a contemporary Cuban science fiction author provides an interesting source for exploring the situation of contemporary Roman Catholic ecclesiology. At a time when the church remains in its own special period, and the moral authority, the adherence of the faithful, and the reliability of the church as a social force for good are threatened, Catholics find themselves in a crucible not unlike Claudia's. Should they stay and collaborate on some level with an institution that all but abandoned the laity in the sex-abuse and cover-up crises because they hunger for the sort of communion Catholicism can provide, or do they set off into the unknown, as Claudia ultimately decides to do?

Moreover, and in a different realm (specifically in the field of ecclesiology), scholars have noted that the reception of the Second Vatican Council remains incomplete and a subject of contention within the church, with competing narratives struggling to control its interpretation.[5] Will the church's mission and identity be defined in a top–down way, where static principles of perfection are defended at the cost of distorting the real, lived experience of the people of God? Or will a more dialogical model hold sway?

Catholics hunger for new ways to articulate the reality of the church more accurately, even if this means that ecclesio-

---

5. See McBrien, *Church*; Richard Gaillardetz, *The Church in the Making: Lumen Gentium, Christus Dominus, Orientalium Ecclesiarum* (Mahwah, NJ: Paulist Press, 2006); John O'Malley, Joseph Komonchak, Stephen Schloesser, and Neil Ormerod, *Vatican II: Did Anything Happen?* (New York: Continuum, 2007).

logical narratives will be less uniform. But who will speak
for, with, and on behalf of the people of God? Espín's desire
to theologize the laity takes place in a hermeneutical context
that this novel helps illuminate. Where do the different stake-
holders in the ecclesiological conversation stand vis-à-vis
the power relationships operative in the different contexts of
church, academy, and society?[6] Lastly, in what ways can the
ecclesiological conversation include the various and pluri-
form voices that make up the people of God and the theological landscape? As we attempt to refocus ecclesiology away
from the exclusive perspective of the religious elites, what
ecclesiologies emerge from contexts and subjects that lie outside the sight lines of the magisterium's "official" story?

In Chaviano's story, Claudia's decision to leave Cuba is
fraught with otherworldly experiences, out-of-body moments,
and multivalent symbology that intertwine the past with the
present and future. The novel, like much of Chaviano's work,[7]
is imbued with Christian symbolism, from the moment of
the dedication of the story to Hildegard of Bingen. The use
of biblical imagery in the subheadings of the novel, as well
as the quasi-liturgical intertwining of music and the sacred
throughout the book, contributes to its mystical themes.
This intertwining of Claudia's near-constant contact with
otherworldliness and her desperation can be seen to parallel the eschatological situation of the people of God—caught
between the already and the not-yet, wrestling with difficult circumstances, seeing no truly "good" solutions, and
at the same time maintaining/embracing the mystical and

---

6. This notion of the publics of theology is David Tracy's. See *Analogical Imagination*.

7. For a sampling of Chaviano's work that touches on Christian
symbolism and other strains of Caribbean mythos see her "The
Annunciation," trans. Juan Carlos Toledano, in *Cosmos Latinos: An
Anthology of Science Fiction from Latin America and Spain*, ed. Andrea L.
Bell and Yolanda Molina-Gavilán (Middletown, CT: Wesleyan University Press, 2003). See also the work of scholars such as Robin McAllis-
ter, Yvette Fuentes, Raquel Romeu, and Maribel Tamargo.

contemplative strain in Christianity, a strain that can never be uprooted from notions of context, time, place.

What makes the novel particularly apt as a source for the contemporary historical moment in Catholicism is its focus on language and silence. Claudia is articulate and jovial; her alter ego, La Mora, is silent. Many of Claudia's hallucinations are auditory as well as visual, but el Indio is silent when he appears. Claudia's ecstatic experiences transport her to times and places that are at once foreign and familiar. This is not unlike the theological task, which interrogates a Catholic Tradition that spans centuries and cultures and creates a kind of palimpsest, so that even though we tell new stories as theologians, they are rooted in the past and written in new ways only in order to convey the prime/central message of the gospel to the contemporary church. One of the goals of theology, then, can be stated as the maintaining of identity-in-signification when it comes to Christian doctrine, and the expressions used to achieve this identity in meaning are as fluid as Claudia's personas, as the landscapes of the novel, and as the apprehensions of the men who love her. John O'Brien states this principle of ecclesiological signification in a moving way:

> A new narrative transmitting a new synthesis is always possible, because narratives and the words that construct them, always have around them a "circle of the unexpressed" drawing the conversation into the "infinity of the unsaid"—surely a desirable scenario for any ecclesiological narrative that wishes to communicate how the infinity of God's love is at work among God's people. One important corollary of this reading is the realization, at once humbling and liberating, that after us will come people who will understand and articulate what we hold dear, in a more adequate manner than we do.[8]

---

8. O'Brien, "Ecclesiology as Narrative," 156.

Ecclesiology must be particularly attuned to language and silence, as it attempts to give voice to the self-understanding of the people of God in its racial, cultural, linguistic variety while remaining faithful to the gospel. At the same time, all theology should strive for humility, with the awareness that language, imagery, and insights neither dominate nor contain the reality of God or of God's people. The analogical imagination that guides Catholic theology, including ecclesiology, captures this dichotomy of language and silence. The theologian knows she must say something, and at once knows that anything she says is insufficient to the reality of God and the reality of the people of God. This can lead to paralysis, or to freedom of the kind O'Brien notes: the freedom that comes from knowing that one's inadequacy can always be remedied, recapitulated, remapped. The communal nature of the theological and ecclesiological tasks has never been more crucial than in this work of reconfiguration and remapping. Like all scholars, ecclesiologists rely on one another to work toward an adequate expression of a transcendent reality: the nature and mission of the church. When we use literature as a theological source, we see that this communal task can be dialogical and hermeneutical. Here, the methodological insight of Latinx theology, to write and reflect *en conjunto*, seems specifically the method to accomplish this reorienting of ecclesiology from the ground up.

The Triads—Literary Trinities as a Source for Ecclesiology

The triad that makes up the title of Chaviano's novel, *el hombre, la hembra, y el hambre,* translates roughly to "the man" (or mankind/maleness), "the female" (or femaleness), and "hunger." Each of these can be overlaid with ecclesiological significance, both because they represent a fresh perspective on ecclesiological roles in the church, and because the triadic structure fits well with the trinitarian impulses of Catholic theology.[9] If one follows the obvious referent and conceives the literary triad configured like a triangle, the sides would represent the characters, actors, or subjects, and the angles or points of the triangle represent areas of possible convergence or conversation between the subjects.[10] Each part of the triad *hombre, hembra, and hambre* is an abstract noun, but their connotations are not equivalent. There's a power differential embedded in these words that reflects the patriarchal structure of society. *Hombre,* and its use as "mankind" denotes the sort of androcentric understanding of reality in which men are inherently more human than others. *Hembra* stands linguistically in contrast to the natural parallel of *hombre,* which would be *mujer.* Akin to "female" when used as a noun, *hembra* carries with it more subhuman, animalistic connotations, as it in fact is predicated of girls, women, and nonhuman female animals and is the preferred descriptor for livestock. Interestingly, the male equivalent to *hembra* is *macho.* Of course, it's possible that Chaviano chose these nouns because they are alliterative and almost identical save the rearranging of their vowels. Nevertheless, the difference between an *hombre* and an *hembra* is significant because it mirrors the patriarchal milieu in which the story takes place (and, arguably, that still characterizes most of Western cul-

---

9. Some Latino/a theologians who engage aesthetics and the work of thinkers like Hans Urs von Balthasar include Alejandro Garcia-Rivera, *The Community of the Beautiful: A Theological Aesthetics* (Collegeville, MN: Liturgical Press, 1999); Michelle Gonzalez, *Sor Juana: Beauty and Justice in the Americas* (Maryknoll, NY: Orbis Books, 2003); and more recently Roberto Goizueta, *Christ Our Companion: Toward a Theological Aesthetics of Liberation* (Maryknoll, NY: Orbis Books, 2009).

10. I am cognizant of the problem of overreliance on convergence, consensus, and harmony that thinkers like Jürgen Habermas and Jean-Luc Marion point out is inherent in this sort of hermeneutical configuration, and want to emphasize that the goals of these triads of conversation are not necessarily convergence but are open to conflict stemming from the profound problem of power dynamics, especially within Roman Catholicism.

ture including the Catholic Church). By using *hombre* in contrast to *hembra*, Chaviano indicates the subjugated status of the feminine, as well as the elevated, public status of the masculine. This divergence contributes to an understanding of the hermeneutic difference between space and place.

The first subject in Chaviano's triad is *hombre*. In the novel, this can be read to mean humanity in general, in the sense of "mankind," or "humanity" in an abstract, idealized sense. It may also mean the male characters in the book—not merely man in the abstract sense, but also certainly men—the duality of the men Claudia/La Mora has loved, along with el Indio, the silent but forceful representative of the violent past of colonialism.[11] The male characters represent a deductive or reductionistic gaze—an outsider's apprehension of the novel's central character and her identity as either a shy but talented woman of letters or as a silent, damaged prostitute. Rubén and Gilberto introduce the reader to Claudia; their impressions of her, almost entirely sexual even though Rubén also clearly loves Claudia, frame our initial understanding of the main character. El Indio, a third *hombre* in the text, is a powerful male character that is a harbinger of doom as well as a frightening, if familiar, presence in Claudia's life.

The notion of *el hombre* demarcates not only the general notion of mankind or all of humanity, but in a specific way the representatives of a legitimate and easily identifiable "proper place" (which some theorists call a *lieu* in French or a *lugar* in Spanish[12]) throughout the book. The notion of proper place connotes an official, established position of power,

---

11. See Ennis Edmonds and Michelle Gonzalez, *Caribbean Religious History: An Introduction* (New York: New York University Press, 2010). It is also important to note that "el hombre" remains a Cuban euphemism for the Castro government, and certainly was in the 1990s when Fidel Castro was still the political leader on the island.

12. M. de Certeau, *The Practice of Everyday Life* (Berkeley: University of California Press, 1984).

one that has the potential for cultural, spiritual, and physical dominance, even violence, as evident in the scars on the Indio's body. Ecclesially, this aspect of the triad would be the bishops or the magisterium, the official teaching arm of the church, because the magisterium retains (and periodically reasserts) its role as the bearer of the "official" or standard views of the Catholic Church. In terms of the public face of the church, the magisterium (here I mean priests and bishops) are the religious virtuosi—those religious elites charged with meaning making and interpretation of texts, symbols, and rituals. This role, like any official position of power, harbors the potential for violence in a variety of forms, whether through the silencing of voices or cultures, the intellectual violence of creating a single "official" story, or even the potential violence of the procedures by which the magisterium exercises its function as the church's teacher. Like any *hombre*, the magisterium serves a public, outward-facing role in the church.

In contrast to the role and place of these religious virtuosi stands a variety of constituencies in the church, including academic theologians, lay ecclesial ministers, and others whose vocations provide them some space within the church that is not an official, public place or role, but more of a supporting, background persona. Claudia/La Mora is the *hembra* in the title of our novel—the mother and *jinetera* with multiple identities. Her self-identity is fractured in part because of the context in which she is forced to live/work, and the setting from which she ultimately flees in an attempt to rewrite herself once again. Claudia is a fan of role playing and theater, and while La Mora is more than a role for her, it is this ability to disassociate from a part that enables her to survive financially, emotionally, and spiritually.[13] The *hembra* in the story, she is named in a somewhat dehumanizing way that echoes

---

13. Maribel Tamargo, "Hipertexto, ciudad e historia en *El hombre, la hembra y el hambre*: una reflexión," *Confluencia* 24, no. 1 (Fall 2008): 183.

her life and the economic downturn that has dehumanized her, forcing her to turn to sex work when her job as an academic proves useless in her survival. There are parallels, in terms of the difficult economic reality of higher education at present (though the prostitution aspect is a clear identifier of the special period in Cuba), but ecclesially the *hembra* character sparks interesting insights about the nonpublic ecclesial actors in the church and the spaces they occupy in ecclesiology and in the people of God.

In ecclesial terms, one of these actors might be the academic theologian. Academic theology as a vocation is increasingly lay and female. Moreover, academic theologians, in particularly lay theologians, navigate strange terrain. They must steer between their lay identities, which afford them little voice in church matters, and their training and expertise, which give them plenty to say in those same ecclesial matters. Theologians live and work in the interstices: a natural space (*espace/espacio*, as distinct from a *lieu/lugar*, which denotes proper place) between the lived experience of the people of God and the production and interpretation of doctrine.

Academic theologians might be said to occupy their own *lieu/lugar* in the academy, but because as laity they normally lie outside the decision-making structures of the church, they occupy a bifurcated space between the laity and the hierarchy. Nor can we say that the vocation of the academic theologian lacks the potential for violence of its own—intellectual and hermeneutic violence, the temptation of uncharitable reading, the temptation to compete in order to survive in the increasingly fraught world of the church and of higher education. Nevertheless, the lay theologian in particular occupies a nondominant place in the church, which we can juxtapose with the feminine *hembra* in this narrative triad. The feminine connotation of *hembra* makes even more sense since many theologians have begun using the terminology of bearing witness to birth or birthing to describe their role vis-à-vis the experiential turn in theology.[14] Serving as midwives bringing forth new insights from the people of God in dialogue with the gospel, the theologian occupies a feminized space. As a result, one can see the ecclesial role of the academic theologian as one that keeps that space between clergy and laity open as a place where power and lived experience meet.

El hambre functions as a third character in the novel, the extenuating circumstances of the *período especial* in Cuba beginning in 1994, an excruciating period of economic and psychological lack, precipitated by the collapse of the Soviet Union and the drying up of the financial resources that bolstered the economies dependent on the superpower. This period of economic struggle drove Cuban residents to extreme measures like those undertaken by Claudia/La Mora in the text. While clearly not a human character, hunger undergirds the entire text, serves as the impetus for the plot, and grounds the characters' actions. The experience of lack functions as a limit-experience, an experience where one is pushed to the point where one's life is reoriented in a fundamental way. *El hambre*-as-limit-experience pushes people to move beyond imagined possibilities; this is exemplified in Claudia, who moves beyond her academic life to a different form of existence as survival, and encounters different realities as a result of her hunger. *El hambre*, then, represents neither proper place or assumed space, but a hybrid of those two realities, a *lieu-espace* or *lugar-espacio*, the stage on which the narrative takes place.

---

14. J. B. Metz's theological task can also be partly identified with the midwifing of narratives. See J. Matthew Ashley, *Interruptions: Mysticism, Politics, and Theology in the Work of Johann Baptist Metz* (Notre Dame, IN: University of Notre Dame Press, 1998). Ada María Isasi-Díaz is one example of a Latina theologian who describes her role as one of midwifery; see especially *En la lucha/In the Struggle: Elaborating a Mujerista Theology* (Minneapolis: Fortress Press, 2004), and *La Lucha Continues: Mujerista Theology* (Maryknoll, NY: Orbis Books, 2004).

Ecclesially this *lieu-espace/lugar-espacio* is the lived reality of the whole people of God, which can be said to be undergoing its own *período especial* right now, precipitated by the loss of moral authority, which many ascribe to the scandal of sexual abuse and the clericalism that enabled, and in some cases continues to enable, the obfuscation of justice within the church. But this scandal is not the only context in which the church has lost ground. One can point to the increasing irrelevance of the church to young people, the strengthening of secularism, and antireligious sentiment in general as contributing factors to the particular historical moment in which the church finds itself. Rising tides of populism and a lack of response from religious elites in the North American context exacerbate the comparisons here.

No part of the triad is complete in itself; neither is one necessarily the criterion or the condition of the possibility of the other. While the vectors on this hermeneutical triangle of *hombre-hembra-hambre* and its ecclesial cognates seem distinct, it is important to note that the magisterium and the theologians are not necessarily two completely distinct groups, nor do either of these stand outside the "people of God" as a whole at any point; they merely have particular ministries within that people and in the service of that people. Just as the *hombres* or Claudia cannot be separated from the milieu of hunger in the novel, neither do the bishops and the theologians stand outside the people of God. Nor are the people of God merely a background or a context, but they are the church itself, the proper object (and subject) of ecclesiology. It is precisely because ecclesiology focuses on the faith journey of the people of God in history that narrative and hermeneutical theology are uniquely suited to it.

Reading Chaviano's novel generates insights about the lived reality of the church, and how best to understand it. As a theological source, this novel speaks to us about the interrelatedness of the magisterium, the laypersons who serve particular roles in the church, and the daily life of the whole

people of God. Using the hermeneutical categories of space
and place, we see that while the official magisterium of the
church has long held the proper public place of Catholicism
in the world, increasingly the presence of nonordained, lay
academic theologians is bringing forth new possibilities for
exchange between the religious virtuosi and the religious
masses. Much like how women's increased participation in
the public sphere opens up new possibilities for men and
women in a patriarchal culture, lay theologians occupy a
crucial space in the church, as midwives who coax new realities into being because of their dialogical position between
officialdom and the populace. One theologian who specifically thinks of her work as midwifery, Ada María Isasi-Díaz,
uses the categories of place and space in her theological mapping of Havana.

Isasi-Díaz's Map of La Habana: Theological Cartography and Ecclesial Unity-in-Globality

Ada María Isasi-Díaz's essay "La Habana: The City That
Inhabits Me" takes up the issues of space and place in similar ways to Chaviano, though through a theological lens.
Analyzing this text alongside Chaviano's novel allows us to
see the potential for symbiotic dialogue between theology
and literature-as-source.

Like Chaviano, Isasi-Díaz was a Cuban-born woman
living in the diaspora. Their disparate dates of migration
and ultimate locations (Chaviano emigrated in the 1990s
to Miami; Isasi-Díaz settled in New York sometime in the
1970s) do not seem to affect the affinity both women have
for discussions of space and place. Both the novel and Isasi-
Díaz's essay provide the reader with literary maps, in some
cases describing the city of Havana street by street. Isasi-
Díaz, like Chaviano, traverses not just physical space but
time periods as well, as her verbal remapping transports her
to her childhood in Havana. Where Chaviano's literary mapping takes on the character of a palimpsest as it maps and

remaps Havana while traversing disparate historical periods from the colonial era to the present, Isasi-Díaz's more closely resembles a recognizable Havana, at least to contemporary Cubans and Cuban immigrants living in the diaspora. Isasi-Díaz's goals certainly differ from those of Chaviano, but because we are reading Chaviano as a theological source, both authors' literary maps can be seen as outlining important ecclesiological themes. Chaviano's mapping and remapping, along with Isasi-Díaz's recreation of the Havana of her youth, call to mind the plurilocality of the church along with its multicultural character. They sensitize us to the difficulty of maintaining unity in this fundamental diversity, and, through their exploration of particular/specific spaces and places, these authors highlight new ways of thinking about a global church that respects particularity while forging bonds of unity based on attention to those most in need.

Isasi-Díaz's essay, while not a literary narrative as such, nevertheless serves as a particularly useful companion piece not only to Chaviano's novel but to the task of this book as a whole. Methodologically, Isasi-Díaz structures her essay by beginning with the retelling of particular stories of specific Latinas and their relation to their homelands. This grounding in particularity animates Isasi-Díaz's essay, the scope of which is anthropological and ethical; but it is a method that is also at work ecclesiologically in this chapter and this text as a whole, which posits that only through embracing particularity through narrative can ecclesiology fruitfully reflect the reality of the people of God. With a sincere accounting of the reality of the church, ecclesiologists along with the magisterium can ensure that ecclesiological models, as well as doctrinal efforts and plans for mission (visions of the church *ad intra* and *ad extra*, respectively) are viable for the church today.

Isasi-Díaz centers her essay, which reads very much like a memoir, on a theological anthropological understanding of Latinas as "multi-sites, displaced persons."[15] Echoing the insights of many Hispanic theologians about belonging nei-ther to the dominant U.S. culture nor to the Latin American ancestral homeland,[16] she writes: "For economic or political reasons, either as migrants or refugees, Hispanas/Latinas have had to leave our places of origin—abroad or in the USA—to look for another place to call home," and later, "Hispanas/Latinas are always 'on the move,' creating a constant 'from there to here' that results in living in many places but never fully being at 'home.' This 'from there to here' is also part of our multiple, shifting identities, a fluid social ontology that is one of the constitutive elements of *mestizaje-mulatez*, the racial-ethnic-cultural-historical-religious reality that is the *locus* of the Hispanic/Latino community in the USA."[17] Here, Isasi-Díaz could easily be describing Chaviano's protagonist, Clau-dia, in her bifurcated identity, or this understanding could be extended to the notion of *la hembra* as a whole. Note Isasi-Díaz's shift from the historical fact of migration to the anthro-pological-ontological awareness of not-belonging. This is significant for the self-understanding of all displaced persons, not merely Latinas, though it is interesting that it appears in such a parallel fashion in Chaviano's and Isasi-Díaz's under-standings of Hispanic women. Rather, this awareness of not-belonging can apply to all people, especially in the Christian worldview that includes a vision of the human as a both-and of material and spiritual reality, of sin and grace, of cross and resurrection, history and eschatological hope. Thus, the state of in-betweenness named by Latinx theologians applies well to Christian notions of personhood and by extension to the

---

15. Ada María Isasi-Díaz, "La Habana: The City That Inhabits Me. A Multi-Site Understanding of Location," in *La Lucha Continues: Muje-rista Theology* (Maryknoll, NY: Orbis Books, 2004), 126.

16. Authors such as Virgil Elizondo and Roberto Goizueta have written poignantly on this topic. See especially Goizueta's account of bifurcated identity in *Caminemos con Jesús*, 1–17.

17. Isasi-Díaz, "La Habana," 127.

church, which is at once a historical and spiritual reality, participating in the already-but-not-yet character of Christian salvation—even facilitating that salvation as a sacrament, as the first chapter of *Lumen Gentium* states.

Not surprisingly, given the experiences of migration that feature so prominently in explorations of Hispanic identity, Isasi-Díaz moves to ground this anthropological insight in the notion of physical location. She describes the utopian project of mujerista theology (her term is *proyecto mujerista histórico*) as geographic: "Hispanas/Latinas' *proyecto histórico* has a geographic base: we were displaced from somewhere concrete and our 'original' selves—our first selves as well as our creative selves—continue to be displaced not only from where we were but also from where we have arrived or have always been."[18] For Isasi-Díaz, wherever Latinas work to make their utopian dreams of a society that excludes no one a reality, they are always already engaged in creating new space. I believe this is a way for Isasi-Díaz to ground her at times florid utopian notions in historical reality. Her vision of the future can be described as a place where in-between-identity is constitutive of reality ("includes where we come from and where we are").[19] Geographic location, both in origins and present location, makes a person who they are, and thus the future created by those persons must necessarily involve a geographic component as well.

The overlap with Chaviano's novel is clear and visible throughout. Claudia's struggle with multiple identities and multiple selves epitomizes the displacement to which Isasi-Díaz refers. Displacement and multilocality describe Claudia/La Mora's predicament and her reaction to her bifurcated reality. What Isasi-Díaz's insights do is redeem this reality, and make it a privileged perspective in creating a utopian future. We must not ignore the critical mass

18. Isasi-Díaz, "La Habana," 128.
19. Ibid.

of Latinas who make up the Catholic Church in the United States, or the central role of Latinas in passing on religious traditions within Christianity as a whole. Thus, the church in the United States is made up, in significant portion, of the sort of people described by Chaviano and Isasi-Díaz—it is a displaced church, made up in large part of people Isasi-Díaz calls "multi-sites persons" who live in the interstices of cultures. This ecclesial diversity of place/space is not limited to the American context. It did not develop with the migration of Latinas or even with the era of colonization that brought so much more cultural diversity into Christianity. Rather, the multi-sites reality of the people of God has been constitutive of the church from its beginnings. It is scripturally codified, as seen in the Pentecost event, where each visitor to Jerusalem heard the kerygma in culturally intelligible ways.[20] Historically, too, the church flourishes globally in a variety of cultures, as it must. The challenge of identity-in-signification regarding the gospel across geographic, linguistic, and cultural divides forces us to think creatively about how the church is a multi-sites reality. Isasi-Díaz and Chaviano suggest potential avenues, including the church as palimpsest and the church as an example of globality.

Isasi-Díaz spends the bulk of her essay describing the city of Havana almost street by street, particularly with reference to its significance to her life story. She meticulously outlines the geography of the city and lingers on the sites that mean the most to her personally and to the country's history: the seawall of el Malecón, the tomb of Antonio Maceo, the Plaza de la Revolución. This careful reconstruction of the city enables her to stay in touch with the reality of her life, but also with the reality of a country whose history did not begin with the communist revolution in 1959 or end with the author's migration. The city itself, in its geography and in Isasi-Díaz's descriptions of the difficulties people in Havana

---

20. Acts 2:6–11.

struggle with in terms of transportation and meeting basic needs, demands that the reader/observer take stock of the multiplicity of meanings and histories that make up this metropolis.

Like Chaviano's magical-realist palimpsest, Isasi-Díaz's literary mapping forces the reader to broaden the lens through which she views the city, the country, and the people of Cuba. Isasi-Díaz's mapping guards against the nostalgic idealization of "home" that comes from living in exile: "Space and time—distance—make us long for what we have known, tricking us into thinking that the past was better than the present, and insisting that we hold on to what was. As a countermeasure we need to stay in touch with what is in our communities/countries of origin and not just with what was by reinserting ourselves there as often as possible."[21] By keeping in continuous contact with our places of origin and the multiple locations that make up our identity, Latinas guard against the temptation to idealize reality, ground themselves in the complexity of the historical moment, and are thus able to forge a liberative future that excludes no one, as Isasi-Díaz suggests.

I would argue that the literary remapping performed by Chaviano and Isasi-Díaz serves as a model for ecclesial narrative as well. In forcing ourselves to tell the real story of the real church, we guard against false idealizations of the past or dangerous generalizations about the present. When we accurately re-present events through honest storytelling, we see not only the complexity inherent in the present ecclesial moment but the diversity and complexity that have characterized a community throughout history. Like Isasi-Díaz's mapping of Havana then and now, storytelling in ecclesiology allows for fidelity to the real lived experience of the church. Narrative ecclesiologies, and the theological cartography they involve, yield space for dangerous mem-

21. Isasi-Díaz, "La Habana," 131.

ories to be unearthed, to flourish, and to disrupt idealist narratives of what the church has been, is, or should be. In traversing these stories and maps, we see that the church has always been characterized by diversity in worship, in theological formulation, and in pious practices, and that the unity of the people of God has never been contingent on strict doctrinal or confessional uniformity (which would be impossible to enforce, given the global reality of the church throughout history).

The task for ecclesiology, made easier by the work of thinkers like Isasi-Díaz, is first to map the multi-sites reality that is the church and then to use that map to ensure that the kerygma continues to be heard in ways that are both culturally intelligible and doctrinally stable. Narrative ecclesiology does not mean an anarchic undoing of magisterial authority. Instead, it makes plain the ways in which authority functions in the church: not as a top–down series of decrees, but frequently as the confirmation of the intuitions and actions of broad swaths of the people of God. This "bubbling up" understanding of authority ensures cultural intelligibility and doctrinal stability. The both–and task of ecclesiology is rooted in the both–and identity of the church and in the already-but-not-yet character of a community that lives in eschatological hope.

Women's Work

A final insight of this treatment of literature as theological source has to do with the choice of women's work—literature by women and theology by and about women's work—to highlight the *sensus fidelium* and the proper space and place that should be allotted to lay insight, and women's insights especially, in the church and the academy. It is no secret that women's work and indeed women's lives have historically been trivialized, marginalized, undervalued, and relegated to the private sphere. Women's full humanity, even just their ability to open a bank account or pursue graduate studies or have a career of their choosing, was up for debate in the United States until the middle of the twentieth century and remains so in many parts of the world. That women's artistic and literary production has historically been relegated to the realm of the nonprofessional, the craft artist or niche writer, is unsurprising. Even Daína Chaviano's recognition as a "popular" author diminishes her scholarly import. Reading and writing for women has been portrayed as something that is done purely for leisure, not for impact. Women's intellect has historically been viewed as geared toward men's entertainment, as when women were encouraged to read so they could be interesting conversation partners. The use of art and literature by women as a source for theology advances our ecclesial conversation in two ways: it elevates women's work by recognizing it as the church's work, and it brings theology and especially ecclesiology into the realm of *lo cotidiano*, the everyday reality that is women's lives (and, really, human life). To trivialize the work of women, whether their household work or their literary production or their academic achievement, belittles the people of God. Moreover, the hermeneutical triad of theologians/magisterium/people of God needs women's voices, not because they offer some particularly "feminine" insight but because without these voices, one cannot claim to speak of the fullness of the reality of the people of God.

Latinx theologians have long noted that women do much of the pastoral work of the Catholic Church, despite not being ordained clergy. How much is owed to older faithful women as guardians of the faith—custodians of the *sensus fidelium*? Espín writes eloquently about this in his essay "An Exploration into the Theology of Grace and Sin."[22] There he centers

---

22. Orlando O. Espín, "An Exploration into the Theology of Grace and Sin," in *From the Heart of Our People*, ed. Orlando O. Espín and Miguel H. Díaz (Maryknoll, NY: Orbis Books, 1999), 121–52.

"mature Latina women" (by which he means older women, married and unmarried, frequently stereotyped as the *abuelitas*, or grandmothers) as the fundamental, privileged interpreters of grace as well as the mediators and victims of patriarchal sin and violence. In the context of an essay on the theological anthropological realities of sin and grace, Espín highlights the ways in which older Latinas, by virtue of their roles at the centers of families, function as the protagonists of *lo cotidiano*, the everyday reality that is a locus of theology. "Mature Latina women give us life and nourish it among us. . . . [They] . . . are also our families' wise interpreters of the biblical message and of the heart and mind of God, the teachers of ethics, and the leaders of our prayers, our family's living sacraments of God and the sacred."[23] If theologians are to take seriously the experience of *lo cotidiano* as a theological source, then the role of mature Latinas is paramount to this discussion. Neither are Latinas relegated only to the private sphere that one might assume *lo cotidiano* denotes. Rather than a private reality, the everyday is social and communal, public and cultural in that it denotes the lived experience of humanity in a particular context. In the Latinx context, older women dominate this sphere because, as Espín notes, they are the ones with whom Latinx persons "sustain the most meaningful and deepest of daily relationships."[24] They are the mothers and grandmothers, whether biologically or not, who give life and nourish it, who sustain life, and who are responsible, according to Espín for "the survival and resilience of popular Catholicism."[25]

One might conclude that in naming mature Latinas as the central figures in the Latinx experience of *lo cotidiano*, Espín is in effect feminizing, and therefore marginalizing, a vital contribution made by Latinx theology to the global church. To

---

23. Espín, "Exploration into the Theology of Grace and Sin," 128.
24. Ibid., 128.
25. Ibid.

assume this would be a grave error. In fact, much of Espín's theological project involves arguing for the centrality of *lo cotidiano* as the primary locus theologicus that grounds all other theological insight. In all his work, especially *The Faith of the People*, Espín makes the case that popular expressions of faith, particularly of popular Catholicism, while not unique to U.S. Latinx populations or to Latin America, nonetheless represent the key theological insight of Latinx thought, because popular Catholicism undergirds many, if not all, the theological insights in this community. These faithful expressions of the people of God do not just amount to exotic rituals on the margins of Northern European "magisterial" Catholicism, which has been construed as the norm. Instead, popular Catholicism expresses, for Espín, realities as fundamental to Catholic theology as the Incarnation, the Trinity, and the interplay of grace and sin. When he emphasizes the role of mature Latinas in prayer, ethics, family, and religious imaginary, as "empowerers and bearers of cultural identity in our lives,"[26] Espín subverts the patriarchal tendency to view women's work as marginal and feminization as disempowering. Quite the opposite. His acknowledgment of the centrality of women in the process of cultural and religious traditioning (he would not separate these two, as a forerunner in the understanding that all religion is necessarily culturally inscribed and experienced) demonstrates how women's work is religiously central, not theologically marginal.

It makes sense, then, that this study would take up women's literary and artistic work as central to a reimagining of the church's story. Authors such as Ferré and Chaviano, artists such as López, and theologians such as Isasi-Díaz, all mature Latina women, are attuned to *lo cotidiano* in their communities and represent it in their work in varying ways. If everyday sacred reality, where God encounters humanity, is aptly interpreted and described by women, it is also

---

26. Ibid.

characterized by women's reality as what Isasi-Díaz calls multi-sites persons.

Along with the indispensable work of catechesis, prayer, and traditioning highlighted by Espín, we should also acknowledge the multi-sites reality of women's lives as envisioned by Isasi-Díaz. As women struggle to integrate the demands of the public/private sphere, living in these multiple sites is becoming increasingly common in the United States regardless of one's sex or gender. We know that identity is composed of a variety of contexts; interculturality and hybridity are the norm and not the exception today. At a time when U.S. cultures are struggling with what to make of marriages that are leaving behind gender stereotypes, of women in the workforce in large numbers demanding equal pay and trying to "balance" the varied demands on one's time and attention, a multi-site existence seems a good way to reimagine anthropology as well as ecclesiology. The "work" of the church—prayer, community, devotion, and social action—happens in many divergent places for Latinx Catholics, as we will see in a later chapter. Christians are multi-site people, as Latinos/as have pointed out for years of living "on the hyphen" or in-between cultural identities. Increasingly, then, we must push for a multi-sites church, present in people's lives and meeting them where they are, like the field-hospital approach suggested by Pope Francis. Like the lives of Christians, the church, too, ought to be a multi-site reality, creating unity out of a plurality of contexts, cultures, languages, and perspectives. One can also envision the *sensus fidelium* as a multi-site reality. The example of Ferré's and López's Guadalupan portrayals highlights this aspect of the sense of faith. Despite geographic separation, both envision Guadalupe in similarly nontraditional ways, as a powerful, active woman who helps those who "fight for what they want." The church, then, can be a multi-site reality, holding within itself the pastoral and the doctrinal, the liturgical and the sacramental, the doctrinal and the transcendent.

Highlighting women's work allows women to take our proper place at the table, recognizes women's contributions ecclesially and ecclesiologically, and enriches our understanding of the ecclesial debt owed to women's fidelity. But not only that. To focus on women's work also overcomes a lack in ecclesiology methodologically. Women have largely not participated in the discussions that bring about doctrines about the church or any other aspect of doctrinal theology. Moreover, lifting up women's work contributes to our understanding of the importance of the pastoral work of women, this work's centrality to ecclesiology. Lastly, attentiveness to women's work reminds us of the necessity of hearing insights about the gospel and discipleship from every corner of the church, not merely the official channels. As Pope Francis forms a commission to study the history of the female diaconate, it's important that we see that women's pastoral work has gone on in the church, often unrecognized (and nonordained/nonvowed) but no less critical to the church's thriving, especially in places where ecclesial infrastructure and clergy were lacking. Women's intellectual work, their artistic work, and their pastoral work all contribute to the edifying of the people of God.

Foregrounding the work of women enriches ecclesiology in several ways. First, we are reminded of the importance of the pastoral, the day-to-day discipleship that constitutes the story of the church and is the foundation of any genuine ecclesiological reflection. Second, we lift up key players in the life of the church whose work has been marginalized and trivialized, rendered insignificant. Third, we achieve important insights about the multi-site, hybrid reality that is the nature of the church in which, as *Lumen Gentium* states, the kingdom of God subsists and which should be a sacrament of salvation. That salvation cannot come about without the pastoral, intellectual, spiritual, and ecclesial work of women.

Concluding Thoughts

Literary narratives can be crucial components of contemporary ecclesiology. When approached as a resource for theology, these narratives bring to light divergent strains of popular religious practices, attitudinal shifts in people's understandings of doctrine, and the reality that all doctrinal expressions, prayers, practices, political stances are culturally bound even as the God that grounds the church and the Spirit that enlivens it are not. The *sensus fidelium*, that infallible sense that belongs to the whole people of God reaffirmed by the Second Vatican Council, cannot be understood apart from explorations of popular religious practices such as those detailed in literary narratives such as Ferré's essay.

Ecclesiology can also approach literary narratives as a source, finding in diverse aesthetic narratives profound insights about human relationships, self-awareness, community, and society connatural with the doctrinal impulses of Catholic Christianity. The narratives analyzed above, all of which focused on the wisdom of Latinas as multi-sites, displaced persons navigating a global reality, point to the importance of integrating literature into theology. Chaviano's text highlights the hermeneutical triad that functions in narrative ecclesiology of the sort John O'Brien advocates, and brings out some of the complex power at work in the discernment of the *sensus fidelium* and the production of doctrine. Isasi-Díaz's work of mapping, of grounding narratives in places and spaces, heightens our awareness of the church as a multi-site, global reality in history. Together, these texts indicate how literature doesn't serve merely as a data mine for theologians who can scour stories for people's religious understanding and/or practices. Though this work represents one important function of literature in theology, the spark of insight that comes from reading literary texts that reorient our relationship to our reality makes literature as source a truly viable conduit for theological exploration.

Ecclesiology should seek to narrate the story of the people of God, systemize these stories, and harmonize them with the story of salvation in Christ. Enlivened by the Spirit, the church continues to be a sacrament of salvation. However, we come to know God and God's salvific activity better by knowing more closely the story (and stories) of the people of God. Like cartographers, ecclesiologists must survey the landscape of the polycultural, multilinguistic, socioeconomically diverse church and see the Spirit at work in it. This cartography can happen from above, but it can be truer to reality if it is done on the ground. Ultimately, the "big picture" of a narrative ecclesiology turns out to be a mosaic of smaller stories, culturally bound narratives of necessarily culturally bound encounters with the living God. The narratives in this chapter point the way for this cartography, and Latinas stand at the forefront of this work. Much like mapping, land surveying and cartography describe what is really there—the lay of the land—the integration of narrative into ecclesiology helps create a dynamic portrait of the real church, from which we can move confidently in the direction of the eschatological, promised ideal.

In their growing awareness of the centrality of popular religious practices, especially popular Catholicism, as well as in the retelling of the narratives of colonialism, exile, migration, repatriation, documentation, and alternative documentation, Latinx theologies refashion the story of the people of God. These narratives are not an end in themselves, but represent a crucial first step toward accountability to the majority of God's people (the lay poor). Ideally the narratives also return, systematized in a variety of ways, and remain accountable to that people through the methodologies of Latinx theology that retain a rootedness in the communities that call us forth.

The reassertion of the pastoral not as the endpoint in a deductive chain that begins with ideal principles of ecclesial reality (*communio, perichoresis,* even subsidiarity) but as the summit and the source of the task of ecclesiology places Latina/o theologies at the forefront of contemporary narrative ecclesiology. By taking seriously the biographies of and within our communities Latino/a theologians retell the story of the people of God, not in a definitive way but in a way that attempts to draw together, to synchronize and harmonize, even if these efforts do not necessarily succeed. Like Chaviano's novel, the narratives alternate between the worldly and the otherworldly; they are bifurcated and polyvalent, rich in symbolism and imagery that need not always be coherent or harmonious. In fact, the discord produced by the articulation of previously silenced stories or the re-articulation of communal and spiritual violence can be productive itself. As Isasi-Díaz reminds us, the ultimate utopian project, which I have interpreted ecclesially to be the eschatological reality of the church, is born in the interstitial places occupied by those on the margins, like Latinas and many other displaced persons.

At the end of Chaviano's story, Claudia winds up on a raft with her son, David, as well as with Rubén and Gilberto immediately after a very awkward moment of recognition between the three adults. The men realize in this final scene that the woman they've spoken so much about is one person. The reader knows Claudia has chosen to leave behind the island that has occupied so much of the novel and so much of Claudia's emotional, psychological, and spiritual life. Driven by hunger (both physical and psycho-spiritual) and desperation, they set out, confused but together toward the unknown, the whole triad on a flimsy raft that may capsize. This image of discord, fragility, and also of solidarity provides inspiration for the future of Catholic ecclesiology. As the church and the world stand at a precipice in history, a time of great hunger for justice, for integrity, for peace, will the self-understanding of the people of God find adequate expression in ecclesiological work? Will we be able to build an ecclesiology that is born from and accountable to the church's pastoral reality, which is inductive, often discordant, and in those ways reflective of the complexity of the church in the twenty-first century? Can we, by telling the stories of the worlds in which the people of God live, give insight into the rich symbolic, historic, sometimes violent reality of the church? With attentiveness to the everyday, by focusing on the richness of popular religious devotion, and a willingness to inhabit a context that is ever changing and complex, it is my hope that our work as Latinx theologians will point the way to a hope-filled future for the people of God.

CHAPTER FOUR

Cuenta conmigo
Demographic Narratives and Ecclesial Structures

Literary narratives can produce ecclesiological insight when approached as a source, and they can serve as a treasure trove of artifacts of the *sensus fidelium* when viewed as a resource for ecclesiology. Similarly, historical narratives help ecclesiologists shape a vision of what is possible in the church in light of what has taken place in the past. History can preserve dangerous memories, and thereby foster alternative tomorrows for the church. Demographic studies and ethnological narratives also aid in constructing an ecclesiology from below. This is because the field of demographics helps scholars get a sense of the scope of reality, the contours of people's lives, their opinions, affiliations, and preferences. Though the study of the church could never be reduced to polling data, nevertheless information from censuses, surveys, and opinion polls proves valuable when assessing what religious practices endure in Catholic communities, as well as which practices are growing or waning with the passage of time. Demographic data tell us how people understand themselves in the present and give scholars a snapshot of a society as it exists in the present. Armed with this knowledge, ecclesiologists can discern what theological or structural frameworks might best serve the flourishing of the people of God now and into the future.

At present, demographic studies from the Pew Research Center and the Center for Applied Research in the Apostolate (CARA) indicate that the religious landscape in the United States is shifting away from institutional religion, including a sharp decline in Catholicism, especially among millennials, half of whom will leave the Catholic Church.[1] This trend to disaffiliation has contributed to the decline and reorganization of U.S. parishes, whose waning numbers mean financial crises that warrant the closing of some churches and the combining of others. The data paint a picture of a deteriorating church. But what motivates people's departure from institutional religion? Can we discern broad social trends for or against some characteristics of the Catholic Church that help us imagine how the church might flourish in the present cultural context? What resources exist in the tradition for reimagining the way the church could function in a secular, pluralistic society such as ours?

One important characteristic revealed by demographic data concerns disaffiliation from institutional religion. In the second decade of the twenty-first century, sociological studies and surveys on religion have shown that an unprecedented number of people, especially the young, no longer identify themselves as belonging to a particular religious tradition. The phenomenon of the rise of the "nones" chronicled by think tanks such as Pew and authors like Kaya Oakes (among others) reveals an unprecedented demographic shift

---

1. Both the Pew Research Center and CARA (Center for Applied Research in the Apostolate) conduct polling and present social scientific data on many facets of contemporary life, including the current religious landscape of the United States and other countries. The Pew Research Center, affiliated with the Pew Charitable Trusts, is a think tank based in Washington, DC. CARA is also based in Washington, DC, and is affiliated with Georgetown University. Its work focuses on trends within the Catholic Church.

away from organized religion and toward some uncharted new reality.[2] This exodus has understandably caused great anxiety in the church, an anxiety intensified by the closing and restructuring of parishes all over the country because of fiscal shortfalls and population shifts that have rendered many church buildings financial burdens on their dioceses. Add those who are disaffiliating because of apathy or doctrinal disagreement to those who are left homeless in the closing and restructuring of parishes, and the numbers of former Catholics start to make sense. The upheaval felt by Catholics forced to leave behind the places most spiritually significant for them, where they celebrated sacraments, milestones, births, and deaths understandably makes it seem as if Catholicism in the United States is in the midst of a rapid, unstoppable demise.

Amid the doom-and-gloom forecasts of the downfall of all organized religion, and Catholicism specifically, Latinos/as have consistently been cited as a source of hope for the future of the church in the United States. While it is true that new immigrants from Latin America buoy the statistics and make it seem as if a Western-European style secularization trend doesn't exist in the U.S. church, more recent studies show that Latinx Catholics are showing similar patterns of defection, both in the direction of secularization (nones) and toward Pentecostalism.[3] It would be naïve to ascribe the defection of Hispanic Catholics to the same causes as non-Hispanics. This ignores the very real differences not only within and among Hispanic cultures but also the ways in which the experience of Catholicism varies depending on language, culture, immigration status, and location of a com-

---

2. See Pew Research Center, "America's Changing Religious Landscape," http://www.pewforum.org, as well as analysis by CARA, http://nineteensixty-four.blogspot.com, among others.

3. See especially the CARA analysis, which identifies millennials and Hispanics in a trend away from weekly Mass attendance and strong religious affiliation.

munity in the United States. Furthermore, lumping Latinx Catholics in with their non-Latinx coreligionists erases the phenomenon of Latinx Catholicism entirely, with its particular characteristics stemming from the history of the Ibero-American encounter and the legacy of colonialism, which continues today. To complicate this further, one can speak of a variety of Latinx Catholicisms, as each community's experience of and with the church varies geographically, linguistically, and in relation to the community's circumstances of migration. An immigrant or exile community arriving in this country in a relatively short time period does not experience U.S. Catholicism in the same way as a mission community in the Western United States that was annexed during westward expansion. It is imperative, then, that we look closely at the complex history and the varied expressions of U.S. Latinx Catholicism in order to understand the phenomenon of disaffiliation and the motivations that might be at work in these defections. We would do well, too, to search the tradition for successful expressions of Catholicism, particularly of Latinx Catholicism, given the trend (still holding, for now) toward Hispanicization in the U.S. church. These successful Latinx Catholic expressions might speak to the cultural moment the broader U.S. church traverses right now.

After a brief analysis of the current demographic situation of Catholicism in the United States, this chapter investigates the roots of Hispanic Catholic defection and alternative affiliation, finding that key characteristics of Latinx Catholicism are crucial to understanding this community's interaction with the dominant ecclesiological paradigm in the United States, including the trend toward disaffiliation. Motivations for Latinx disaffiliation seem to lie at least in part in a combination of the Iberian Catholic worldview of Latin America and the failure of the territorial parish model in the United States. Then, using the work of Ken Davis and other theorists, I argue for a nonterritorial model of parish life that shows promise for promoting ownership and leadership in the contemporary church, as exemplified in the model of the Agrupación Católica in Miami, as well as other Marian sodalities and Christian Life Communities (CLCs). This model incorporates the demographic narratives of Hispanic Catholicism, which reveal a decentralized church that is less reliant on the geographic parish and more on bonds of friendship, spirituality, and politics. Further, the model embodies a lay-focused ecclesiology for the third millennium. For Pope Francis, this messy church where the laity shakes things up (*hacen lío*) in the world shows promise in an increasingly secularized, anti-institutional culture.

Ecclesial Snapshot: Demise, Disaffiliation, DIY Religion

The Pew Center on Religion and Public Life published a report in 2015 documenting the rise of a group they termed the "disaffiliated": people who identified themselves as belonging to no particular religious tradition. This unaffiliated group, known colloquially as the "nones," comprised nearly 23% of American adults and is growing rapidly.[4] The news for the Catholic Church is quite dire; Pew found that the retention rate for Catholics to be only 59% (that is, 41% of Catholics no longer identify as such), and project that half of all Catholics in the millennial generation will leave the church. One in two young Catholics will eventually join the nearly 14% of all Americans who identify as "former Catholics." This is obviously very distressing, and the causes of this decline in religious affiliation are unclear. Some speculate a general anti-institutional sentiment; others blame the moral teachings of Catholicism regarding sexuality as being outdated and irrelevant to young people. Still others claim that the loss of moral high ground as a result of the sexual-abuse crisis and ensuing cover-up is the reason for the spike

---

4. Pew, "America's Changing Religious Landscape," chap. 2.

in disaffiliation or deconversion from Catholicism. Whatever the reasons, which are surely complex and interrelated, the growing presence of religiously unaffiliated Americans and the substantial number of former Catholics in that group should be cause for concern for all Catholics, and especially for theologians who study the church.

In 2011, ecclesiologist Richard Gaillardetz characterized the state of contemporary U.S. Catholicism as one marked by the demise of the "American Catholic subculture," by which he meant the end of "ethnic Catholic enclaves" in major cities in the United States toward the end of the nineteenth century.[5] Other scholars have similarly noted that the national parish, where successive waves of immigrants from Europe would arrive in the United States and together build a church that was ethnically homogenous with liturgy in the mother tongue, was an untenable model. At the turn of the century, the U.S. church was moving away from ethnic enclaves of Irish, Italian, or Eastern-European immigrants and toward a more centralized, geographic model of church governance where parishes were multicultural—to an extent.

As the U.S. church faced the beginning of the twentieth century, Catholics of a variety of ethnicities were assimilating into North American culture. Indeed this was the accepted model for new immigrants: to leave behind the language and customs of their homelands and become "fully American."[6] The U.S. Catholic Church was no exception,

---

5. Richard Gaillardetz, "State of the Church, 2011: Reflections on the State of American Catholicism Today," *National Catholic Reporter* March 1, 2011, https://www.ncronline.org.

6. Assimilation was facilitated (and incentivized) by the distance between the United States and Europe and the difficulty of returning to the homeland. When some migrants left Ireland or Italy, they did so fully aware that they would not return. This is not the case for immigrants from Latin America, connected to the states by a border shared with Mexico. Moreover, technology and travel have advanced so that immigrants needn't fear they will never see their homeland again.

and as its numbers swelled and its members assimilated, the perceived need for ethnic enclaves declined, as Gaillardetz notes. Additionally, the American government's decision to implement new immigration laws and quotas slowed the flow of immigrants from Europe, stabilizing the U.S. Catholic Church somewhat, and allowing Catholics to gain economic and political footing in the country, though they remained a minority faith. The rise and fall of the ethnic parish, then, coincide with the waves of immigrants from Western Europe, whose clergy frequently migrated with them and facilitated the growth of ethnic enclaves, particularly in the Northeast and Midwest.[7] When that influx died down to a trickle, Catholics reorganized into more heterogeneous, geographic, "melting pot" parishes, and the American Catholic ethnic enclaves diminished.

For many Latinx Catholics, the story differs. An uptick in immigration from Latin America and the Caribbean coincided with the U.S. church's geographic reorganization and the abandonment of the ethnic parish model. Ken Davis writes that national parishes functioned as havens for European immigrants, who "from a position of strength guaranteed by a parish that respected their language and culture, . . . were successful in becoming a vibrant part of the church in the United States of America."[8] Hispanic Catholics, on the other hand, irrupted into the national consciousness after the abandonment of the ethnic parish model, because the very success ethnic parishes had afforded their European-ethnic communities meant the dispersal of those populations out of one geographic enclave and into other urban and suburban areas. As European immigrants assimilated, they moved to the suburbs and out of the urban enclaves, leaving

---

7. Kenneth Davis, "Built from Living Stones: Hispanic Parishes without Boundaries or Buildings," *New Blackfriars* 88 no. 1015 (2007): 335–52, 337.

8. Ibid., 348.

behind "vacated church complexes that ultimately became fiscal liabilities for local dioceses."[9] Instead of being encouraged to build their own Catholic ethnic enclave parishes, immigrant Latinx Catholics were urged to become part of already-existing territorial parishes. However, Latin American immigrants lacked the financial and ecclesial resources to build their own ethnic enclaves in most cases. Many of these new immigrants were poor and uneducated, in addition to being of mixed legal status, so that navigating the creation of ecclesial communities within the territorial parish system in addition to figuring out housing, work permits, and the like was prohibitively challenging.

Furthermore, these new immigrants lacked ecclesial resources because of the general dearth of native clergy in Latin America. In many cases, the complex relationship of the church in Latin America to colonial powers, namely, their cooperation with or silence in the face of the oppression of the poor, exacerbated the reasons for migration from places like Nicaragua and Mexico. Without clergy to lobby for their interests in the ecclesial sphere, and without money to buy land or build structures for their ethnic parishes, Latinx Catholics were, in many cases, shoehorned into parishes where they were viewed as outsiders, usurpers, or invaders.[10] Met at times with outright hostility and at times with conflicted situations where parishes were only beginning to chart their own paths as multicultural realities,

---

9. Ibid., 348.

10. It is important to note that there are exceptions to the lack of Hispanic ethnic parishes. These exceptions, like the Iglesia de San Juan Bosco in Miami and others in San Francisco and Detroit, are highlighted by Gerald Poyo and Timothy Matovina in their treatment of the shift away from national parish models. See the introduction to Part 3, "Crossing Borders: The Immigrant Experience," of *¡Presente! U.S. Latino Catholics from Colonial Origins to the Present,* ed. Timothy Matovina and Gerald E. Poyo (Maryknoll, NY: Orbis Books, 2000), 95–96.

Latinx Catholics found that they did not quite fit in to the U.S. church as neatly as they did at home.

Today, as the U.S. church confronts the reality of deconversion and the rise of unaffiliated Catholics, as well as the financial burden of decaying church buildings resulting in parish closings and mergers, we must explore new models of being church. There is evidence that intentional communities, volunteer opportunities, and other meaning-making experiences function much like "church" for some now-unaffiliated former Catholics. Might U.S. Catholicism be moving toward a new model of church less focused on the geographical parish and more on familial, emotional, ethnic, and spiritual ties?

Kaya Oakes, a Berkeley-based religion writer, recently published an extensive study of the phenomenon of unaffiliated Americans, the "nones." There, she outlines the phenomenon of Do-It-Yourself or "DIY" religion, in which young adults who no longer belong to a parish or attend Mass nevertheless participate in meaningful communities and experiences, usually centered around social justice, for their spiritual fulfillment. Many of Oakes's subjects feel alienated from the church, abandoned or exiled, but still seek out community, social justice, and spirituality in their daily lives through careers, volunteering, and political action. Oakes writes: "They still wanted what the church should have provided: community, consolation, the palpable presence of God. When they were told they didn't fit in, they may have stopped attending mass or changed the way they practiced their faith, but they still felt, and identified, as Catholics."[11] She continues: "even though Kyle and Maria [two of Oakes's subjects] were exiled, they were still a part of the church. They wanted the binding. So rather than waiting around [for structural institutional change], they became DIY church,

---

11. Kaya Oakes, *The Nones Are Alright: A New Generation of Believers, Seekers, and Those in Between* (Maryknoll, NY: Orbis Books, 2015), 171.

for a DIY generation, in a time of DIY religion."[12] While Catholic ecclesiologists might not go as far as DIY religion, there are elements of the do-it-yourself-church that could work, and indeed might already be at work, in the current ecclesial landscape. Although polls show sharp losses in Catholic affiliation and strong gains among the unaffiliated, there is evidence that the search for religious meaning has not waned. For example, Pew found that many former Catholics still believe in God,[13] and find spirituality important. Should the church not endeavor to harness this energy? Would ways of affiliating that move beyond geographic boundaries and parish buildings provide an element of do-it-yourself-ness that appeals to unaffiliated millennials and also incorporate traditional Catholic practices and communal models?

U.S. Latinx Catholicism: Anomaly in Disaffiliation or Strategy for Resilience?

The U.S. church is evidently in flux. We see it in the struggles to keep parishes open, the consolidation of parishes and the closure of others that are not financially viable. Urban churches flounder while suburban churches boom in some places; in others, even suburban communities suffer closure and mergers. The sense of loss among people whose parishes have closed shouldn't be underestimated. It leads people away from the church, or at the very least makes it difficult to continue regular attendance at Mass given the greater distances that families must travel, the challenge of integrating into a new worship community, and whatever

---

12. Ibid.

13. Pew Forum on Religion and Public Life, *Faith in Flux: Changes in Religious Affiliation in the U.S.* (Washington, DC: Pew Forum, 2009), 27. A graph illustrating former Catholics' main reason for leaving the church showed that very few (4 percent of the now unaffiliated, and too few to count of those who joined other Christian churches) did so because they "no longer believe in God/Jesus."

sentimental ties a person has to the sacred spaces they had come to know. Emotional attachments to places of worship are very real, even visceral, aspects of the geography and materiality of faith. If we broaden our view to include the ranks of the unafilliated, and the "spiritual but not religious," there are many Catholics and former Catholics in this country who have been alienated from parish life by diocesan reorganizations. History tells us that this alienation from parish structures is not unique to the contemporary period. Some U.S. Catholics have been rendered peripheral to parishes through ecclesiastical reorganization, but others have made their spiritual homes on the periphery, worshiping outside closed sanctuaries, or in homes or alternate locations where the same community can continue to gather. One such peripheral experience of Catholicism finds its roots in the earliest traces of Catholicism on the U.S. mainland: the Latinx Catholicism of the West and Southwest, with its Iberian roots. Iberian Catholicism was characterized by pre-Tridentine qualities such as an emphasis on local devotions and a lack of concern with geographic parish structure. Like some of Oakes's subjects, these Catholics practiced spirituality outside traditional parishes, away from formal liturgies, but no less intensely than other Catholics.

Latinx Catholicism emerged as a visible force in the second half of the twentieth century, in a U.S. church that was itself in great flux, moving away from the ethnic-parish model that characterized the assimilation process of European migrations of the early twentieth century. Of course, the history of Latinx Catholicism in the United States begins centuries before, preceding even the formation of the nation, as the oldest diocese in the country (San Juan, Puerto Rico) was established in the sixteenth century. Still, Latinx Catholics, their pastoral needs, and ecclesial influence have been on the radar of U.S. ecclesiology only since the 1960s and '70s, when the *Encuentro* processes began, as detailed earlier in chapter 1. The uptick in Latin American

migration, along with the increase in Latinx Catholic influence, coincided with broader demographic shifts in the
United States. In particular, shifts in immigration patterns
and legal restrictions, as well as ecclesial changes meant
to solidify the American character of the Catholic religious
minority that was the U.S. church, left many U.S. Latinos/
as adrift in terms of finding spiritual homes in their territorial parishes. Latinos/as relied on relationships other than
those that made up a geographical parish for their spiritual homes: family ties, nationalism, personal friendships,
political affinity. When we speak of the phenomenon of
disaffiliation from Catholicism, we must not exclude U.S.
Latinx Catholics, because they are also leaving the church,
whether to join Pentecostal communities or become part of
the ranks of the unaffiliated. Nevertheless, it would be sim-
plistic to attribute the defection of Latinx Catholics to the
same reasons cited by the Pew study or Oakes to be moti-
vating non-Latinx Catholics. Instead, there is some fruitful
overlap to be found between those former Catholics Oakes
interviewed who were engaging in DIY religion and U.S.
Latinx Catholicism's various strains of popular religious
practices, and this overlap should be examined.

Latinx Catholics differ from non-Latinos in their motiva-
tion for disaffiliating in that they tend to disaffiliate toward
either no church or Pentecostal communities. The reasons
for this are inevitably complex, as history, colonialism, racism, and religiosity intertwine differently in the wide variety of cultures that make up the U.S. Latinx reality. But we
can isolate some characteristics that make Latinos/as' religious practices different, and help explain to what extent and
why this group of Catholics takes part in the trends toward
deconversion and disaffiliation.

First, the experience of Latinx Catholics in the United
States amounts to a clash of cultures between groups accustomed to being the majority religion (in Latin America) and
the minority faith that Catholicism has always been in this

country. Second, we must account for the prevalence of nonliturgical or extraliturgical piety in Latinx Catholicism, which is rooted in some characteristics of the Iberian Catholicism that colonized the Americas. Third, we should attend to the ramifications of the low numbers of native clergy in Latin America (even today), and how this lack of clergy affects Catholic practices and influence in home countries and in the United States as a host country. Lastly, the Latin American phenomenon of small Christian communities based not only or primarily on geographic proximity but on family, friendship, and political ties means that U.S. Latinx Catholicism includes a variety of small, lay-led communities similar to the small Christian communities (SCCs) that are already functioning in the United States. The Cursillo movements, a variety of Jesuit ministries, prayer groups with devotions to particular saints or Marian apparitions are just a few examples of these.

One common characteristic of Latin American Catholicism, as Kenneth Davis points out, is that it has always been a majority religion: "even without sufficient clergy, it (Catholicism) remained vibrant because it permeated all of society" through popular devotions that characterized people as Catholic and Hispanic at the same time.[14] When, through migration, the majority religion of Latin America comes into contact with Western European–style U.S. Catholicism (rooted in Ireland, Italy, Germany, etc.) that immigrated to the Northeast and Midwest as a minority religion fighting against anti-Catholicism, conflicts are inevitable. The racial politics of the United States exacerbate these conflicts, along with the demographic realities of Hispanic Catholicism, including rampant poverty, a dearth of native clergy, and the resulting lack of influence this cultural group had on mainstream U.S. Catholicism. As a result, the prevailing ecclesial paradigm in U.S.

---

14. Davis, "Built from Living Stones," 337.

Catholicism comes mainly from its European component and less from its Latin American roots. But this paradigm has largely excluded Latinx Catholics, or relegated them to church basements as parallel communities within a parish still dominated by Euro-Americans. The numbers show that the Euro-American paradigm is dying, as all models eventually do. This process of the decline of a paradigm is natural, and need not be a catastrophe. The paradigm can be mourned and then moved beyond. If the church seeks to move forward in the third millennium in the United States, it must change tactics, not necessarily or exclusively through the consolidation and closure of parishes but by broadening its scope, taking into account the extraparochial tendencies of Latinx Catholics, and those of the unaffiliated as well.

It may be impossible to discern whether U.S. Latinx Catholicism features so much nonliturgical piety because of the relative lack of clergy in Latin American history or because of the Iberian Catholic roots of this region. Iberian Catholicism emphasized local devotions and deemphasized parish life, rendering clergy less important and therefore fostering the flourishing of extraparochial practices. In either case, the relationship between a lack of native clergy in Latin America and the blossoming of popular religion that exists on the periphery of parish life and/or in homes is symbiotic. If there are not enough priests because you live in a rural area, or if the priests are all Spaniards or criollos and you are indigenous or mestizo/a, maybe they don't fully understand you culturally. Maybe the clergy is aligned with a colonial government or oligarchy that oppresses you. In either scenario, if the priest doesn't "get" you, you might supplement worship and spirituality with devotions at home or somewhere else outside the official parish. If the Catholic DNA in Latin America, Iberian Catholicism, already included a propensity to favor local devotions and not parish life, then this tendency makes all the more sense.

Racialized colonial church politics in Latin America meant that for much of its history, a country's Catholic Church might be led by a European bishop. Because the European settlers often viewed the indigenous natives and the African slaves as subhuman, access to the seminaries for these groups, as well as their paths to ordination, was long and arduous at best. A further consequence of the low numbers of native Latin American clergy is that when immigrants arrive in the United States, very few priests migrate with them. This not only presents a problem for establishing ethnic Catholic churches, but also reduces the influence of Latinx Catholic immigrants in the U.S. ecclesial landscape.

Why did so many Latin American immigrant waves arrive without a substantial amount of Catholic clergy to minister to them? The colonial reality of Latin America provides some answers here. Aside from the historically small amount of clergy available in Latin America (due, in part, to the refusal of European colonizing clergy to ordain indigenous and native men to the priesthood), the sheer number of people and geographic dispersal of populations in Latin America meant that many Catholics had limited access to the clergy, especially if they were located in rural areas. For example, Ana María Díaz-Stevens remembers her childhood in rural Moca, Puerto Rico, as follows:

> Religion in that mountain town of my childhood was part of daily life despite the fact that some of us saw the priest and visited the town church sparingly . . . each member of the family should at least go (to church) the one Sunday a month assigned to the sodality to which one belonged. For the girls in the family it meant inviting all the girls from the neighboring farms to sleep over. It also meant getting up before the crack of dawn . . . walking miles to the paved road (crossing two streams of water on the way) and then boarding a *público* [public transportation vehicle], in which we

literally felt like we were packed in a can like sardines. This was a three to four hour expedition.[15]

Many Catholics in Latin America lived similarly isolated from the sacraments, and this, coupled with the local-devotion-heavy Iberian Catholicism brought by the colonizers, enabled the traditions of popular Catholicism to blossom into the rich reality we see reflected today in U.S. Latinx processions, *posadas*, home altars, and other public and private practices. Despite the overwhelmingly Catholic character of Latin America, the catholicity of many of the Latin American immigrants in the twentieth century wasn't tied to the kinds of sacramental practices that one would expect to find in a parish setting with a team of clergy. Latinos/as were accustomed to being Catholic, as Virgilio Elizondo frequently remarked, with, without, or despite the clergy.[16]

Inevitably, then, conflicts about integration into U.S. parish life ensue, and after a few generations, a migration from Catholicism to other religious communities or no particular one might be inevitable. Nevertheless, there is a sense in which these varied but ubiquitous lay-led, popular Catholic practices are a cornerstone of reimagining the church for the third millennium. Might the practices that gained prominence in Latinx Catholicism because of a lack of clergy (in homelands) and were maintained after migrating to this country because of the hesitation of U.S. clergy to welcome Latinos/as into parishes help pave the way for a new ecclesi-

---

15. Ana María Díaz-Stevens, "Immigrant Traditions: The Religion of the Mountains on Fifth Avenue," in *¡Presente! U.S. Latino Catholics from Colonial Origins to the Present*, ed. Timothy Matovina and Gerald E. Poyo (Maryknoll, NY: Orbis Books, 2000), 252–53.

16. Matovina and Poyo, "Introduction to Enduring Communities of the Southwest," in *¡Presente! U.S. Latino Catholics from Colonial Origins to the Present*, ed. Timothy Matovina and Gerald E. Poyo (Maryknoll, NY: Orbis Books, 2000), 56.

ology that is less dependent on parishes and clergy and more on lay leadership and initiative?

Sociologists have suggested that the home-based practices of Latinx Catholics serve to bolster ethnic identity in host countries, and animate ties with the home country.[17] If we understand ethnicity to mean a shared understanding of roots or origin story, religious practices that take place in home countries and continue in host countries contribute to a robust ethnic identity among immigrant communities. This is particularly true if the religious practices can be easily moved from one context to another.

In the case of Latin American migration, church-based practices have proven more difficult to transplant than, to give one example, iconography from home countries. Catholic communities in the United States have historically been wary of immigrant traditions, viewing them as superstitious or unnecessarily exuberant. This was true even of successive waves of European immigrants, as detailed in the work of Robert Orsi, for example.[18] Fortunately, Latin American Catholicism is replete with home-based devotions, byproducts of both the successful inculturation of the church in Latin America (epitomized in the appearance of the icon of Guadalupe, who looks indigenous and is replete with indigenous imagery) as well as the Iberian roots of the Catholicism brought by colonizers to America. Historian David Badillo roots the prevalence of home-based religious practices in the Iberian origins of Latin American Catholicism. He notes that the Iberian Catholicism of the sixteenth century had not received the centralizing reforms of the Council of Trent, which "solidified parish development for the next four centuries and also strengthened the role of the bishop

---

17. Jonathan Calvillo and Stanley Bailey, "Latino Religious Affiliation and Ethnic Identity," *Journal for the Scientific Study of Religion* 54, no. 1 (2015): 57–78.

18. See Orsi, *The Madonna of 115th Street,* for just one example.

in his diocese."[19] Similarly, Trent's standardization of the language of the Mass, the role of the priest, and the function and performance of sacraments was received in spotty fashion, if at all, in the so-called New World. The religion of the conquistadors and of the early years of colonization "was marked by a renaissance of piety and devotion, of monasticism, and of theological learning, a renewed religious fervor felt in the villages."[20] This village faith stood in contrast to how Iberian Catholics and later Latin American Catholics viewed their local church, with devotions that originated in local contexts. Thus "Latin American expressions of fervent piety continue to exist outside the liturgy, including the use of home altars. . . ."[21]

Despite the hundreds of years between Trent and Vatican II, the geographical realities of Latin America and the paucity of clergy meant that the parish model, and the centrality of the liturgy, simply didn't take hold in Latin America (and the mission territories that eventually became part of the United States in the Southwest as well as Puerto Rico) the way it did in Northern Europe, and extraliturgical devotions remain a central part of Latinx religiosity today. This proves beneficial to the creation and retention of ethnic identity, because extraparochial practices (those that happen outside the physical space of the parish church and/or the purview of the local pastor), including home-based practices, can migrate with immigrant communities without the need for approval from the clergy or hierarchy of the host country. The home-based practices and nonparish-based groups, meetings, processions, and sodalities function for Latin American immigrants in a way analogous to how the national parishes functioned for the waves

---

19. David A. Badillo, *Latinos and the New Immigrant Church* (Baltimore: John Hopkins University Press, 2006), xii.

20. Ibid., xii.

21. Ibid., xii–xiii.

of European immigrants in the early twentieth century. Popular religious practices allow U.S. Latinx Catholics who are newly arrived to have a space to worship, in their own language and according to their local customs. Local devotions and processions allow them to network with other Latinx Catholics, easing their transition to a new country without sacrificing cultural ties to the homeland. Moreover, these practices do not require an established parish to host, accept, or condone them; they happen regardless of official church approval.

The extent to which the Iberian Catholic roots of Latinx religiosity manifest themselves varies for a number of reasons, and it is difficult to transpose the experience of, for example, Mexican-American Catholics neatly onto that of Puerto Rican Catholics. Latin American groups are not interchangeable, because their histories, cultural mixes, and experiences of migration vary. Each experience of colonization differed, because what became "Latin America" comprised a great number of indigenous societies that continued to exist to varying degrees and exert influence on the inculturated religion that emerged. Neither should we underestimate the influence of the religious traditions of African slaves brought to the so-called New World. Each country's history of violence and resilience results in unique expressions of Christianity inflected with the native and nonnative cultures that come together to form the alleged New World.

Centuries later, as different countries in Latin America negotiated their independence from Spain, the role of the hierarchy in civil society differs nationally too, as does the relationship between clergy and laity in general, depending on the alliances of the Church in the struggles for colonial independence. There is no 'one size fits all' Latinx Catholicism with uniform practices, devotions, and affiliations. But this need not be an impediment to Latinx participation in building the future of U.S. Catholicism.

An Alternative Ecclesial Model:
Small Christian Communities

Kenneth Davis proposes an intriguing model of ecclesial structure rooted in the church's tradition: the parish as a community of small communities. He views small Christian communities (SCCs) as a "sign of the times" prompting the church to respond in light of the gospel.[22] SCCs could be formalized into the structure of the church if it were willing to designate "personal parishes chartered as a community of small communities."[23] In Davis's vision, geography would not be the primary determinant of a parish, but rather a group that comes together either as a neighborhood, or more likely through other bonds of friendship, a common vision or goal, a common experience such as a group dedicated to some kind of community service. This group would meet to pray and work together, to reflect on scripture, and would be visited by a priest who might be part of the community in friendship to celebrate the sacraments. This "parish without buildings or borders" model rests on the idea of the SCC as the building block of the people of God. Rooted in *Lumen Gentium*'s notion that church communities are built up from smaller groups, this model remains central to a post–Vatican II ecclesiology. Davis finds historical precedent in the model of the personal parish, as well as in the national parishes that predominated in the United States until the late nineteenth century. Resurgent smaller parishes could again provide support for immigrants, serve as a respite from a dominant culture that is inhospitable to newcomers, and help forge bonds based on language and culture. SCCs have functioned in a similar way in Latin America. In fact, for Davis, the SCC merely "give[s] a name to the way Catholics of the Southern Hemisphere especially in rural areas

---

22. Davis, "Built from Living Stones," 342.
23. Ibid., 349.

had almost always experienced Church."[24] We see this rural experience in the anecdote from Ana María Díaz-Stephens above.

Davis identifies the personal parish as a particular example of an ecclesiology based on the model of SCCs. For him, the advantages of this model include the flexibility and versatility of small communities, which enable them to tailor themselves to changing pastoral needs and a mobile population, along with the ability of SCCs to meet in homes or other public places, obviating a diocese's financial burden of maintaining buildings. After all, Vatican II stressed that the church is primarily the people of God, wherever it is located. From a demographic or sociological perspective, the SCC model "allows for integration" with more bilingualism and biculturalism "without assimilation or defensive ghettoizing."[25] The SCC model makes space for nondominant groups to find the support they need in a church setting, while at the same time promoting integration into U.S. society without the suppression of culture. This has shown to be key in U.S. Latinx populations across the country. The SCC or personal parish model thus serves the U.S. Latinx population in much the same way as the ethnic parish model served the successive waves of European immigrants, but without the overwhelming amount of infrastructure necessary, in terms of buildings (and capital), therefore not demanding the impossible from poorer Catholics. Neither does this model need great investment in terms of personnel or clergy, which fits with the demographic reality of the clergy shortages in North America and throughout the world.

Undoubtedly this model presents some challenges, particularly in a U.S. church that has become increasingly polarized and politically fragmented in the last thirty years. Would a personal parish just consist of a group of like-

---

24. Ibid., 339.
25. Ibid., 350.

minded Catholics who feel alienated? If personal parishes are allowed, what is to ensure the unity of the church? Will parishes merely become homogenous, insular groups with a friendly priest to offer them sacraments? Is not one of the central points of the Eucharist to come together at one table despite differences, so that there is neither Jew nor Greek, slave nor free, as in the vision of Ephesians? If this model is put in place in the United States, more fragmentation is possible in a polarized church, resulting in even fewer opportunities for encounter and dialogue. Rather than being the solution to the privatization of religion common to the Northern European paradigm and critiqued by so many U.S. Latinx scholars, the SCC model could exacerbate this privatization, leading to more insular communities that are more resistant to heterogeneity and other moderating influences.

Nevertheless, the SCC parish model is worth examining in full, for three reasons: First, demographic and sociological shifts in U.S. Catholicism call for a shift in tactics, a radical reimagining of how the church functions in this society. As Davis notes, during "the last exodus of Catholics to Protestant churches [in the Reformation], an ecumenical council was called [Trent], seminaries were established, religious orders founded. The church was willing to revisit any ecclesiastic structure that was no longer addressing contemporary needs."[26] The geographic parish did much to unite European immigrants from a variety of cultures and strengthen the voice of Catholics in a majority-Protestant culture like the United States. As this culture shifts toward more recognition of diversity and increasing secularization and deconversion, though, the time has come to revisit ecclesial structures that are no longer addressing the needs of the people of God and search the tradition for those that may. As parishes dwindle in size, mass attendance dips and financial burdens rise, the age of the geographic parish might be coming to a close. We

---

26. Ibid., 338.

may be moving in North America from an American Catholic subculture to a model where American Catholics operate within a variety of subcultures. The key will be sustaining the Catholic identity and practice of this population and stemming the tide of disaffiliation. Integrating alternative models like the SCC/private parish model offers at least a partial solution to the floundering state of the geographical parish. What's more, the SCC model could provide a haven for the present racially toxic political climate in much of the United States. Recent increases in race-based hate crimes, as well as the increasing threat of deportation, have placed U.S. Latinos/as' lives at risk. Small Christian communities can be safe havens or sanctuaries, providing U.S. Latinos/as with spiritual and legal sustenance as they navigate a more hostile North American environment.

A second reason in support of the SCC model lies in its past successes, evidenced recently in Latin America, and through the more ancient roots of small communities in the Catholic tradition. Against those who would dismiss the SCC/private parish model as a novelty geared to isolating those who think alike into spiritual-ideological bubbles stands the example of SCCs in Brazil, El Salvador, and countless other countries where small groups of Christians gather in lay-led groups for Bible study, worship, and mutual support. This is also true in East Africa. "Today, there are over 180,000 SCCs in the nine countries of Eastern Africa (Tanzania has over 60,000 and Kenya over 45,000)."[27] But the model stretches further back into the earliest Christian communities, also small groups of people who gathered to share food and resources and worship together. Thus, the SCC model boasts both recent success and ancient precedent. This is true anecdotally as well, in my experience. Whenever the ques-

---

27. Joseph Graham Healey, "When It Comes to Nurturing Faith, Smaller Is Often Better," *America Magazine*, May 24, 2016, https://www.americamagazine.org.

tion of church belonging comes up at the (Catholic) college where I teach, consistently I've found that the students who remain Catholic churchgoers are the ones who have developed a community of care, either around a shared passion like music ministry or service, or around a particular spiritual practice like meditation or centering prayer. The SCC experience, then, needn't be centered on ideological or political affinity but can focus on action for the common good, on specific modalities of prayer, or some other bond. Naturally, geographic proximity will play a part, but not necessarily a determining role, in the foundation of these communities. Like the bonds of friendship on which they are built, SCCs can survive some geographic dispersal within a city or a region.

Lastly, the SCC model is already in place in many dioceses around the country and around the world. One need only look at the success of the RENEW movement or any number of CLCs in the United States to know that Catholics successfully participate in small communities of worship and that this increases their rate of participation in liturgy and lay ministry.[28] Simply put, the small community keeps Catholics tied to the church by emphasizing bonds of friendship and care, common vision, or common action. Catholic institutions of higher education tend to do a satisfactory job of involving students in groups that combine spirituality and service, as evidenced in groups like the Jesuit Volunteer Corps and its counterparts sponsored by other religious orders. The Ignatian Family Teach-In draws hundreds of high school and college students with Jesuit ties to worship together and engage in political action at its yearly conference. Similarly, organizations like Habitat for Humanity frequently welcome small

---

28. Maria Luisa Iglesias, "Participative Preaching: Laity as Co-Authors of the Homily," in *Preaching and Culture in Latino Communities,* ed. Kenneth Davis and Jorge L. Presmanes (Chicago: Liturgy Training Publications, 2000), 67.

groups of like-minded individuals for service. The hunger for spiritual community exists, and many young adults thrive in small communities during and immediately after college. The challenge for U.S. Catholicism has been integrating these enthusiastic young people into parish life.

To explore this further, I'd like to look closely at one such small community, the Agrupación Católica Universitaria (ACU), which began in Cuba and is the only small community (they identify themselves as a Marian sodality) to have successfully reconstituted itself in the United States after the Communist revolution in Cuba and the ensuing exile of many of the island's Roman Catholics. The example of the ACU links Latin American SCCs with the U.S. context without necessarily sharing the political context of the South and Central American SCCs that are more well known. By using the ACU as a test case, we can see how the tendencies of Latinx Catholics toward extraparochial, friendship-based, and lay-led models of church translate in the United States.

The Agrupación Católica Universitaria: A Narrative History

The ACU presents an interesting test case. Its membership is open only to men, and it remains under the auspices of the Jesuit order, even though it is a legally separate entity. Nevertheless, members of the ACU participate both in common worship and political action, though not necessarily the sort of political action one would see, for example, from a social-justice-oriented group on a college campus in the Northeast. Unlike most small communities known as "sodalities" before the Second Vatican Council, the ACU never moved to identify itself publicly as a "Christian Life Community" (a CLC), but remains a "Marian sodality," perhaps as a sign of the more conservative political and religious views of its membership. Still, the group belongs to the global association of CLCs while retaining its sodalitarian identity. ACU has survived and thrived through a variety of challenges, chief among them the Communist revolution in Cuba and the ensuing exile and dispersal of many of ACU's members across Europe and the Americas.

The story of the ACU begins in the interplay between colonialism, the hierarchical church, and religious orders in the Caribbean. Throughout Latin America, religious orders, particularly the Jesuits, Franciscans, and Dominicans, dominated the ecclesial landscape and, in varying ways, the political arena as well. The pro-Spanish loyalty of Cuban clergy left the island's hierarchy with little influence after the struggles for independence from Spain and then from U.S. occupation at the turn of the nineteenth century. The rebuilding of Catholicism's public image resulted largely from the efforts of religious orders like the Jesuits, the Franciscans, and the De La Salle Christian Brothers, primarily through the founding and support of religious schools. To facilitate this renaissance, "Cuban bishops adopted a laissez faire attitude, giving great leeway to congregations and individuals" in terms of organizing Catholics for worship and social action.[29] Eventually, congregational, ideological, and generational fissures emerged in Cuban Catholicism: in general the clergy was less interested in political activism than the laity, the youth were more vigorously committed to working for social justice, and the Cuban Jesuits embraced Spanish Catholic traditions and political ideals, like those of Fr. Manuel Foyaca (who sympathized with Falangist tendencies in Franco's Spain), while other orders like the Christian Brothers turned to figures like Jacques Maritain for inspiration on how the church could engage the volatile political sphere. The Agrupación Católica emerged from an initiative within the Jesuit order, which ran a prestigious high school (Nuestra Señora de Belén) in Havana. The prefect of this school, Fr.

---

29. José M. Hernandez, "The ACU: Transplanting a Cuban Lay Organization to the United States," *U.S. Catholic Historian* 21, no. 1 (2003): 103.

Felipe Rey de Castro, founded the ACU in 1928, as "a place where university students of Catholic backgrounds could gather to cultivate their spiritual and religious life as they continued their education."[30] The group, made up of young male college students and recent graduates, allowed upper-middle-class Cuban Catholics a space to think creatively about putting their faith into action. "In a society with strong secular traditions like Cuba," writes Gerald Poyo, "Catholic lay movements provided the vehicle for keeping Cuban youth graduating from Catholic schools linked to their faith beyond Sunday mass."[31] It is easy to see the overlap with contemporary U.S. society, with its increasingly secular population and the rise of the unaffiliated and disaffected former Catholics. Moreover, it seems that the problem of keeping young Catholics engaged and active in faith communities has always vexed the church. Lay organizations can play a major role in keeping faith relevant and vibrant—and the ACU provides one example of how this might happen.

Though not the only lay organization operating in Cuba by the second half of the twentieth century,[32] the ACU was certainly among the most visible. In 1958, as frustrations with Fulgencio Batista's dictatorial government grew, along with awareness of rampant poverty and injustice, Fidel Castro's revolution was on the cusp of victory. That year, the ACU published a pamphlet, "Porqué reforma agraria" (Why agrarian reform?), in response to the "disconcerting agrarian situation in the country" and the poverty of *campesinos*.[33]

---

30. Gerald E. Poyo, *Cuban Catholics in the United States 1960–1980: Exile and Integration* (Notre Dame, IN: University of Notre Dame Press, 2007), 14.

31. Ibid., 13.

32. Poyo identifies a number of other groups, including the Federación de la Juventud Cubana (FJC), the Asociación de Caballeroc Católicos de Cuba, Juventud Estudiantil Católica, Juventud Universitaria Católica. Ibid., 13–20.

33. Ibid., 31.

Thus, the group took initiatives in the political realm, but not militarily or in the mode of charity or service. Rather the group's focus was on intellectual conversion, publication, and persuasion. Years later, members of the group, most notably Rogelio González Corzo, would participate in armed resistance to the Castro government. González Corzo was executed by Cuba's Communist government in 1961 and is revered as a "martyr" among the *agrupados*.[34]

The ACU's presence in Cuba allowed its members to take their faith seriously and to use their influence as privileged members of society on behalf of those who were suffering from poverty and unjust land distribution. These aims, while not unlike the stated goals of the Castro revolution, would eventually come into conflict with the emerging communist ideology on the island. As a result, the Castro regime repeatedly attacked the Catholic Church, and the ACU specifically, in the late 1950s and early 1960s, perhaps because of Castro's previous close ties to the Jesuits, as a graduate of Nuestra Señora de Belén in 1944. These attacks culminated in the Cuban government's closure of all lay associations by April of 1961. The Cuban government forced most of the clergy, many active lay Catholics, and all leaders of the lay movements into exile by 1962. This suppression of Cuban Catholicism on the island led to its dispersal into the exile community, concentrated in South Florida, Spain, Puerto Rico, and Venezuela, though Cuban exiles migrated all over the globe.

The church these exiles encountered in the United States, in particular in Miami, embraced an assimilation model of diocesan organization, and refused to allow the new arrivals to form ethnic enclave parishes. This approach seemed strange to the exile community, for whom the parish did

---

34. Material on González Corzo in English is limited to a chapter in a devotional text by Ann Ball, entitled *Faces of Holiness II: Modern Saints in Photos and Words* (Huntington, IN: Our Sunday Visitor Publications, 2001).

not play a central role in their homeland. As historian Gerald Poyo notes, "deeply influenced by a highly activist laity, Catholic life in Cuba revolved less around the parishes than the lay organizations that had regenerated Catholicism on the island. At home, Catholics did not necessarily attend mass in their parish churches, often preferring to attend services with the membership of their lay organizations."[35] For these new immigrants, the diocese of Miami's insistence that they integrate into parishes according to the neighborhood in which they settled, then, was doubly strange. They were accustomed to a vibrant lay community, and were more likely to be compelled to gather by familial, friendly, or other ties (scholastic, work-related, etc.) than by ties to a particular geographic parish. The U.S. model of a clergy-based, territorial system of organization would prove to be a stumbling block for both the immigrants and their host dioceses.

Here the example of the ACU becomes particularly intriguing for elaborating an ecclesiology that takes demographic narratives seriously. Faced with the difficulties of political turmoil, exile, and adjusting to a new cultural and linguistic context, the ACU was able to regroup and navigate a somewhat hostile ecclesial landscape in order to preserve some extraparochial independence and lay leadership. These two qualities, independence from parishes and the need for lay leadership, characterize the demographic moment the church traverses today in the United States. How did the ACU manage its transition from Latin America to the diasporic lands, and how does it function today?

The ACU's transition to the United States resembles the migration of many Latin American Catholics in that it was initially met with resistance and suspicion. In 1962, when the bulk of the Cuban hierarchy as well as its religious orders had been forced into exile, the bishop of the diocese of Miami, Coleman Carroll, reacted as many clerics in host

---

35. Poyo, *Cuban Catholics in the United States*, 93.

countries had: with apprehension at the cultural expressions of Catholicism entering the United States with the Cuban population. Historians have noted that the Anglo clergy in South Florida specifically worried about Cubans' lack of formal religious instruction, their informality, their rejection of clerical control and ecclesial legal structures, and the lack of financial support they offered to their parishes. Monsignor John Fitzpatrick of Miami noted early on that Cuban parents "read very little" and the community seemed lax when it came to regular Sunday Mass attendance. In addition, the Cubans approached the sacraments with a less-than-ideal level of reverence for the Anglo clerics, who observed that the immigrants approached the sacraments for "social rather than spiritual reasons."[36] They arrived late for Mass and for weddings—in short, they disrupted the order of the diocese in a number of ways because of their culturally bound understanding of Catholicism, which did not mesh well with that of the dominant Anglo culture in the diocese of Miami. As Poyo notes, "for Cuban Catholics . . . accepting the centrality and power of the parishes and their priests did not come easily."[37] The history of the Cuban faithful's reliance on and affinity for lay organizations and their suspicion of the hierarchy did not help relations in South Florida dioceses.

For the new immigrants, it seemed that what mattered most was the religious instruction of children—this likely had to do with the fear that Castro, upon appropriating all the private schools in Cuba, implemented a propaganda-based government curriculum, taking education and moral

---

36. Ibid., 91. The bishop's contrast between the social and the spiritual betrays a North American understanding of spirituality as an individual, private endeavor. This understanding necessarily clashes with the spirituality of some Latinx populations, where the social constitution of the human is primary. For more on the role of the social in U.S. Latinx theological anthropology and ecclesiology, see Riebe-Estrella, "Pueblo and Church," 172–88, esp. 174–75.

37. Poyo, *Cuban Catholics in the United States,* 93.

upbringing out of the hands of parents and making children's imaginations, essentially, the property of the state. This fear of indoctrination motivated the creation of Operation Pedro Pan in 1960 and loomed at the forefront of many exiles' motivations for leaving the island. Thus, the education of children, which had been entrusted to religious orders in Cuba, was a main concern for exiles, and lay organizations in the exile communities helped with catechetical formation. Eventually the Archdiocese of Miami was left with little choice but to accept the reconstitution of lay movements, though every effort was made to make these groups accountable to official church channels. The extent to which that oversight worked is best highlighted by historian José Hernandez: "In mid-1968, twelve Spanish-speaking groups were invited to Carroll's installation [as archbishop]. At that time both he and the chancery became aware of a perplexing fact: there were many Hispanic lay groups in the diocese that had sprung up from the grassroots that for the most part were uncontrolled and unrecognized by the official church."[38]

But perhaps no factor contributed to the endurance of the ACU as much as the charismatic Jesuit at its heart during the transition from Cuba to exile, Fr. Amando Llorente. Every person associated with ACU whom I interviewed spoke in glowing, almost hagiographic tones about the priest who first introduced them to the spiritual exercises of St. Ignatius, facilitated their conversion to a more active Catholic faith, and accompanied them for decades on their spiritual journeys. The stories of *agrupados* and their families all seemed to concentrate on the relationship each individual had to Llorente, who died in 2010. In personal interviews and recorded videos, many *agrupados* recall stories of inspirational pilgrimages with Llorente, whether to the Cuban countryside or to the Holy Land. His vision for the group,

---

38. Hernandez, "The ACU," 105.

his leadership and charisma, his humor and deep faith, and his ability to engage young people and keep them enthusiastic about Catholicism and Ignatian spirituality inflected with Ibero-Caribbean tones accounts for much of the ACU's continued presence in the United States today.

Llorente's own life was wedded to the ACU from early in his ministry, and he served the ACU for more than fifty years. Ironically, he taught Fidel Castro while the latter was at Nuestra Señora de Belén in Havana. Later, Castro would exile Llorente and the *agrupados* along with other lay groups, during the purge of Catholic leaders from the island. After arriving in Miami, Llorente remained in contact with the Cuban *agrupados*, and grew the ministry, shifting the vision from one catering primarily to post–high school elite young men to one more suited to the demographics of the early exile: a ministry for young professionals. A motto for the ACU has always been *"un agrupado en cada primer puesto,"* emphasizing that *agrupados* should be at the forefront of business, industry, politics, and social change. Of course, since Llorente was not associated with Belén when it relocated to Miami in 1961, the U.S.-based ACU drew from more diverse pools for its membership. In the United States, ACU was established in Miami, but also had members and chapters in Puerto Rico, Washington, DC, Orlando, Atlanta, and New York.

A second consequence of Llorente's independence from Belén, and perhaps also of the racial-ethnic climate in the U.S. church at the beginning of the Cuban exile, is the ACU's deference to the local ordinary. Many *agrupados* noted the three "pillars" of the ACU: one's spiritual life, one's professional life, and one's apostolate. The primary apostolate, for Llorente, was a man's family, but a close second was service to one's parish. This did not necessarily mean geographic parishes, but rather that each *agrupado* should utilize the spiritual formation he was receiving at the ACU at the service, first, of his family and, second, to the church. The ACU's status as a Jesuit ministry that was nevertheless at home in a variety of dioceses across the United States meant that positive relationships with bishops were key to its survival. It appears that Llorente understood this and saw to it that the *agrupados* not only were business leaders but also were putting their privilege at the service of the local church with the permission and blessing of the local ordinary.

The Agrupación Católica Today

The Agrupación Católica Universitaria continues to exist in the United States, particularly the Southeast, and it attracts members from a burgeoning demographic: young Hispanic professionals. Its central hub is in Miami, Florida, though there are chapters throughout the United States and in Puerto Rico. Though the group does not limit membership on any ethnic basis (boasting that, for example, Cardinal Sean O'Malley of Boston is among ACU's ranks), it remains a predominantly Latino, even predominantly Cuban (now Cuban-American) association.

Membership remains exclusively male, though many of the Agrupación's activities involve families. Women's groups have periodically existed alongside the ACU and associated with it. One interviewee noted that some *agrupados'* wives do the spiritual exercises about once a year. In addition to the women's groups, family-based groups have been associated with ACU since its inception. Moreover, since *agrupados* do not limit their involvement to the ACU, they are visible throughout a variety of ministries in their respective dioceses. *Agrupados* are involved at the parish level, serving on parish councils, as catechists, music ministers, and other ministries, even on a diocesan or archdiocesan level. Many *agrupados* also take part in other extraparochial ministries. Some, though not all, of the *agrupados* are, for example, part of the Catholic home-schooling movement. It seems that Llorente's vision of *agrupados* at the forefront of archdiocesan work has materialized.

Although the Agrupación still seems strong and active in the Latinx ministries throughout the diocese where it operates, the group must currently navigate a delicate transition. The Jesuit who shepherded the group through the early stages of exile and to newfound prominence in the United States died in 2010. After a short series of interim directors, the president of Belén, which was reestablished in Miami in 1961, has been named the director of the ACU. Fr. Guillermo García-Tuñon S.J., a Miami native and 1987 graduate of the school, resembles the pioneers of the ACU in his youth and enthusiasm. But his position and the declining numbers of Jesuits (like all religious orders, and vocations to religious life in general) mean that he must balance his time between running a large Jesuit high school, fund-raising, and traveling with his duties to the ACU. Surely this will be a time of transition. Llorente led the spiritual exercises so frequently that the *agrupados* had the opportunity to do the exercises at virtually any time. Now the group relies on other Jesuits, mainly from Latin America, but many interviewees noted that no one could compare to Llorente. Given that so many men credit him with their conversions, how will the ACU continue to draw committed members?

A second shift in this new era for the ACU has been the sale of the property Fr. Llorente had acquired near Biscayne Bay in Miami. That site had been the ACU's home base, the central meeting place and the location of the annual gatherings of *agrupados*. Under Fr. García-Tuñon's leadership, the ACU will be relocated temporarily to Belén (approximately seventeen miles from the ACU's Biscayne location), while the group seeks out a suitable property near the high school. In addition, García-Tuñon plans to return the ACU to the close ties to Belén that the group had in Havana. Many *agrupados* are excited at the prospect of returning to their roots. This optimism is necessarily tempered by some anxiety about a future without the towering figure of Llorente.

ACU's Impact

The story of the ACU tells us a great deal about lay involvement in the church, especially the involvement of elite, educated members of society in church activity. By no means
is the group exemplary for all ministries or all nonparish-
based action. Rather, the ACU demonstrates one sort of extraparochial activity in which laypeople are deeply invested.
With the structure of Jesuit spirituality and a not-negligible
amount of clerical involvement, the ACU exemplifies one
kind of culturally genuine, socially focused group. In a
homily detailing his plans for the future of the ACU, García-
Tuñon assured the families gathered that the Agrupación
did not exist in the buildings or the (recently sold) property,
in the artwork that *agrupados* had made and donated, but
rather in the relationships the men had with one another
and among their families. Relationship and friendship at the
heart of community building seem to be a key lesson from
the ACU. This sort of relationality, based on common affini-
ties, friendship, even devotion to a particular saint or service to a particular cause, is, to use a biological metaphor,
the cartilage and tendons that hold the church together. The
geographic parishes benefit from a group like the ACU but
by and large do not provide the spiritual fuel these Catholics
need. That spiritual well gets filled through weekly meetings, lecture and study, and liturgy with fellow *agrupados*.
Again and again, in successful small communities, the social
and the spiritual commingle.

Nevertheless, we must not hold up the ACU as the only
model of extraparochial lay involvement. The group has
blind spots, particularly when it comes to the homogeneity
of the socioeconomic class from which it deliberately draws
its members. Focusing on business leaders is a choice, and
it's not one that every group would (or should) make, or even
every Jesuit ministry. Interviewees regularly commented
on the professional success of the ACU's membership. This
emphasis on material success can easily be detrimental to

the spiritual life, particularly if it succumbs to prosperity-gospel thinking. Moreover, the ACU's emphasis on professional success fosters a top–down understanding of social change based on charity, rather than a socially transformative model of justice espoused even by other Jesuit groups, such as the Ignatian Solidarity Group. As a culturally Cuban, even culturally Cuban-exile, group, the ACU reflects many of the idiosyncrasies of that community: quick humor, a love of learning, but also a tolerance for paternalistic colonialism and the underlying racism this colonialism espouses. While not all ACU members vote Republican, the group skews politically conservative, like a large swath of the Cuban-exile community, and so is somewhat politically homogenous. Still, the members I interviewed emphasized that the *agrupados* do not "talk politics," and that there is no ACU "party line" except to follow the church's teachings. If the history of U.S. Catholicism and the present polarization in the church and the nation tell us anything, it's that different interpretations of "following church teaching" are the rule and not the exception. Still, the basis in Jesuit spirituality gives the group a touchstone, ensuring that the unity of the group is based there, and not on political or other forms of uniformity.

Those of us who believe that extraparochial lay groups hold the key to the next phase of the church in the United States would do well to be attentive to the future of the ACU. As the number of Jesuits declines and the number of Latinx Catholics continues to grow, laypeople in groups like the ACU who depended on clerics for spiritual guidance and sacraments will find themselves tasked with new leadership roles and decision-making power. Though the ACU remains a top–down organization, the *agrupados* will soon discover whether they are up to the work of accompaniment and encouragement, and even spiritual counseling of one another. Ultimately, the story of this group offers us some insights about how similar bodies might function in the church in years to come.

Though extraparochial groups form and are fostered by similarity of background or purpose, and are therefore prone to a certain amount of homogeneity, encouraging members to bring their personal, social, and economic resources to existing parish churches helps combat political tribalization. Groups like the ACU that are rooted in the spirituality of a religious order can forge relationships with other ministries sponsored by the order, and grow their faith-networks in that way. But we cannot deny that extraparochial groups like the ACU support and encourage people of faith to be active members of the church, provide a community of friendship and accompaniment, and nourish the spiritual lives of their members. While by no means a prescriptive vision for all lay groups, the Agrupación's story demonstrates one example of a specific (identifying as Cuban exile) cultural group of Catholics engaged in nonparish-based liturgy and reflection. This reflection returns to the parish churches in service. While at one point, perhaps at the height of the American Catholic subculture, groups like the ACU (sodalities, even) may have been housed in geographic parishes and fostered the sort of relationships the *agrupados* speak about, demographic shifts in Catholicism have left parishes ill equipped to do the sort of spiritual accompaniment that extraparochial organizations can.

Conclusion

Lay-led groups, DIY religion, and even the possibility of personal parishes seem to be what the sociological and ethnographic data tell us will succeed in the church's present cultural moment. Of course, these elements are not sufficient for an ecclesiology, but they are a start. The personal parish, while not ideal and not immune to corruption, nevertheless is an intriguing model that could potentially harness much of the energy of young people who seek a DIY spirituality. This DIY sensibility should be balanced, of course, with roots in the long history and tradition of the church, but we should not forget that the history of the church includes testing new paradigms, like monasticism, celibacy, or geographical parishes, when the older ones falter. Lay-led groups are vulnerable to homogeneity and exclusivity. They must be rooted in spiritual practices that have deep roots in the church's tradition. Moreover, these groups should nourish people's faith lives, but be outward-facing, encouraging active participation in the life of the broader church. Lastly, these groups should never stop questioning their own prejudices and presuppositions, and the ways in which their approaches are necessarily partial and incomplete responses to the many needs of the contemporary church. It is through reinforcing, celebrating, and centering the familiar and friendly relationships, the cornerstone of U.S. Latinx anthropology and ecclesiology, that the people of God will continue to thrive.

CHAPTER FIVE

En resumidas cuentas
Narratives and Ecclesiology:
Lessons and Criteria
for Engagement

Many stories matter. Stories have been used to dis-
possess and to malign. But stories can also be used to
empower, to humanize. Stories can break the dignity of
a people. But stories can also repair that broken dignity.
—Chimamanda Ngozi Adichie

The study of the church should tell the story of the church.
Through history and social science, theology and biblical
studies, ethnography and archaeology, we forge the narrative of what it means to be the people of God. Because the
church's story spans ages and continents, theologians make
choices and attempt to prioritize what elements of the ecclesial narrative are most important in a given age and for a
given audience. Too often, ecclesiologists focus on grand uni-
fying metanarratives of the one, holy, catholic, and apostolic
church, leaving the details of how that church functions in
the lives of the people of God as an afterthought. In the wake
of the Second Vatican Council and in particular the reminder
in *Gaudium et Spes* that the church participates in the joys,
hopes, griefs, and anxieties of the whole world, especially the

poor, ecclesiology should make a turn to experience, as portrayed in narrative, in order to systematize the story of God's people. This book represents an initial attempt at such a turn.

This work is not meant to be a comprehensive ecclesiology in the style of Richard McBrien or Richard Gaillardetz. The text is far from exhaustive, nor is it some kind of prescription for the exclusive or proper way to do narrative ecclesiology. It indicates some key inroads that the relationship between narratives and ecclesiology might make; it aims to start the process of a bottom–up ecclesiology that takes seriously the insights of the laity, particularly the silenced and the marginalized. Much has been left out, including seminal literary theorists and theorists of religion and literature. I selected only a few authors and artists, and a central criterion was that they spoke to my experience in particular, cultural, idiomatic ways. These selections are not meant to foreclose future dialogue with other authors and texts. Quite the opposite; this book is a demonstration and an invitation.

It demonstrates the synergy created when we think theologically about stories and storytelling, as well as the importance of particularity, of telling particular personal stories and highlighting those as a place of divine encounter, and therefore as a possible place of ecclesial encounter. In recounting particular stories, we are called out of our own experience and into a shared world—this is a fundamental reality of the *ekklesia* as well. By selecting a few particular stories, telling them honestly, and allowing them to spark ecclesiological insight and inform ecclesiological doctrine, I am inviting you, the reader, to do the same. What stories speak to you? What narratives retell your own experience in someone else's voice? The experience of another narrative resonating with our experience allows us to glimpse the sacred human communion that binds us all. The church should be a place where our individual and communal stories are heard, retold, celebrated in the telling and retelling of the story of Christ's Incarnation.

This brief work uncovered for me a variety of threads that I hope to explore in future writing. The most glaring of these is the need for a more robust analysis of the role of racism and colonialism within and among Latinx communities. The overwhelmingly light-skinned phenotype of the Latin American elite class is reflected in the stories that are published and told, in the art, and even in popular media like telenovelas. This book does not include the thoroughgoing analysis of the ways class and race intersect, for example, in Ferré's story of a young, light-skinned wealthy child and her poorer, likely darker-skinned employee. Gilda's race is never mentioned in "The Battle of the Virgins," but enough is said about class and disadvantage that we can draw important conclusions about the structure of society in the Hispanophone Caribbean. Further, the example of the Agrupación Católica begs for colonial and racial analysis as well, as does any group that is racially and ethnically homogeneous. Even Chaviano, who portrays the plurality of race and class in Cuba in more complex ways, needs analysis to deconstruct the racial and colonial worldviews that inform her worldview. I have taken the narratives in this book at face value, analyzing them on their own terms as examples of how to engage in narrative ecclesiology. The crucial antiracist, decolonial analysis awaits a further research project, and it is sorely needed.

Narrative Ecclesiology:
Enfleshing the Church's Story

John O'Brien reminds us that "[e]cclesiology does not merely read the faith journey of the people of God with the doctrinal tradition; it also reads the doctrinal tradition with the faith-based narratives of that faith journey."[1] Ecclesiological doctrines about unity or apostolicity, about the structure and

---

1. O'Brien, *Ecclesiology as Narrative*, 157.

mission and ministries in the church *ad intra* and *ad extra*, provide the framework for the work of ecclesiology but do not exhaust this work. Rather, ecclesiologists must enflesh this skeletal framework by reading it together with the praxis of Christians, the lives of the people of God. These lives are narrated in history and literature, they are gauged in demographics, they are revealed through ethnography and sociology. A narrative approach to ecclesiology, then, takes seriously the stories encoded by and about the Christian community in all genres, not merely scholarly ones, but also in public and private popular devotion, in art and literature, and in thick descriptions of the lives of individual Christians and their communities.

The challenge for the ecclesiologist is to weave together these two realities. To continue the anatomical metaphor, if ecclesiological doctrine represents the skeleton and narratives the flesh, ecclesiology provides the tendons and cartilage: it binds the body together, bones and muscles; it helps bones move more easily at points of friction; it allows space for new growth; and it lends a pliable structure to flesh, allowing for movement and life. Narrative ecclesiology has the capacity to ease tension in a polarized church climate, because it brings a variety of experiences into dialogue, and guards dangerous memories, preventing them from being subsumed into false histories. This type of ecclesiology provides avenues for the emergence of new ecclesial paradigms because it takes the reality of the people of God into account and returns ecclesial reflection to the pastoral reality that is its most important source. Furthermore, narrative ecclesiology allows for versatility and nimbleness—the connective tissue that keeps our airways open even as it allows us to move our necks and look around us. Telling the church's story (and the church's stories, and even the churches' stories) reveals a far less rigid ecclesial and doctrinal uniformity than many imagine, while at the same time allowing us to draw similarities across communities and historical periods.

This breathes new life into the church, and sheds fresh light on the notion of unity. As *Lumen Gentium* reminds us, unity is rooted in faith in Christ, and in shared participation in the Eucharist, not in exact uniformity of beliefs or devotions.

Narrative, *Sensus Fidei*, and the Value of Connaturality

In order to grasp what it means to reorient ecclesiology from top–down to bottom–up, and thereby to understand how narrative methodologies contribute new understandings to ecclesial marks like unity and catholicity, we must revisit a key theological concept in this study: the *sensus fidei*. This innate sense, or intuition of faith, belongs, according to the ITC, to individual believers (the *sensus fidei fidelis*) as well as to the church as a communal entity (the *sensus fidei fidelium*).[2] Throughout this work I have referred repeatedly to the sense of the faithful as something overheard in literature and art, as something contained in dangerous historical memories as well as in demographic shifts and long-held religious and devotional practices. If we are to theologize the laity, and theologize about the church from the perspective of the laity, understanding the *sensus fidei* is key. The ITC's 2014 document *"Sensus Fidei* in the Life of the Church" provides a helpful guide to the contours of the sense of the faithful, its history in church teaching, and its expressions in the present. The document also offers criteria for discerning the true expressions of this faithful intuition. Taken together with some salient insights from Latinx theology about popular religiosity, aesthetics, and the sense of the faithful, we can begin to flesh out the contours of how narrative approaches to ecclesiology enrich our concepts of church.

Early in their study, the ITC notes that "the faithful have an instinct for the truth of the gospel, which enables them

---

2. ITC, *"Sensus Fidei* in the Life of the Church," 4.

to recognize and endorse authentic Christian doctrine and practice and to reject what is false."[3] This instinct differs from theological reasoning because it is not the result of the deployment of rational categories and procedures but instead is "a natural, immediate, and spontaneous reaction, and comparable to a vital instinct" by which the believer is attracted "to what conforms to the faith and shuns what is contrary."[4] Where does this instinct for the faith come from? The ITC locates the origin of the *sensus fidei* in part in the Thomistic notion of connaturality, by which it means "a knowledge by empathy" or "a knowledge of the heart," over against a knowledge that derives from conscious delibera- tion. The concept of connaturality is compelling because it describes a resonance or attunement between the person of faith and the object of faith, which is Christ. The theolo- gians of the ITC utilize the analogy of friendship to explain connaturality. The relationship between two close friends provides an intimacy that forms the basis of shared natural dispositions between the two persons. Another useful anal- ogy can be found in one's native language and culture. As a resident of New York City, and particularly of the Bronx, home to immigrants from all over the world, I hear many different languages in my neighborhood. Something stirs in me, though, when I hear someone speaking in Spanish, but most especially when that Spanish is inflected with a Cuban accent (or when I hear someone speaking English with that very distinct Miami accent). I can only describe the feeling as one of intimacy with this other, of affinity, love, care, attrac- tion. Hearing your own accent in the voice of an other acti- vates a sense of shared reality: he and I share life somehow; she and I share past or present experience. This feeling of shared reality, affinity, resonance—this is connaturality. It is a combination of attraction and a sense of ringing true.

---

3. Ibid., 2.
4. Ibid., 54.

Connaturality in the sense of the faithful is a gift of faith, but the experience of connaturality can be provoked analogously through a variety of experiences. Storytelling, because narratives intend to resonate with the reader or listener, sparks the sense of connaturality. Seeing ourselves reflected in another, in a character or a work of art, for example, draws us out of ourselves and at the same time rings true within us. We are, at the same time, drawn outward and inward, toward our fellow humans and to a deeper understanding of ourselves. For theologian Roberto Goizueta, building on the work of José Vasconcelos, the aesthetic realm is an important source of creating a sense of unity between persons, which I believe also involves a recognition akin to connaturality. In *Caminemos con Jesús*, Goizueta sets out a comprehensive understanding of Christology, theological anthropology, popular religious practice, ethics, and aesthetics in a U.S. Latino/a key. Anthropologically and aesthetically, Goizueta echoes what thinkers like Ada María Isasi-Díaz and Gary Riebe-Estrella have noted, that for U.S. Latinas/os, community is central to any notion of self, and the individualism prized by the West is in fact quite foreign. "The anthropology implicit in U.S. Hispanic popular Catholicism is altogether different. Here, community is understood to be fundamentally preexistent (therefore involuntary) and constitutive. Therefore the universal is not merely the sum of the particulars; rather, the universal is mediated by the particulars."[5]

Community for Latinx Catholics makes up who we are. It is not added on, voluntarily, as a feature of our existence. Social, familial, geographic, and religious communities are inherent to identity. To think of human beings as isolated individuals forging a path on their own makes no sense in this worldview. Thus, particularity doesn't mean individualism at the expense of community. Particularity here refers to knowing an other as a subject rather than accounting for

---

5. Goizueta, *Caminemos con Jesús*, 65.

people as objects or faceless individuals. One way we come to know others, to experience others as subjects, is through narrative and storytelling.

This is why notions of the church are enriched by narratives like Ferré's or Chaviano's, or art like López's: they expose a particular understanding of the sacred that can be entered into by others, an invitation to appreciate their particular view, and also an invitation to a new understanding of the whole. I worried, in writing this book, that the range of literature I was examining was far too narrow, and that it would not be of much use to the church universally to read a text so focused on the work of a handful of Latinas, most of whom are from the Caribbean. But in fact the opposite proved to be true. When ecclesiologists attempt to account for the whole faith of the whole church, what Goizueta would call modern rationality takes over, and we can come to view the church as a collection of autonomous individuals or autonomous communities, which we can add together into an amalgam of individuals called church.

To foster unity in a church of individuals is quite difficult from this arithmetic approach, and one can see where the anxieties about different practices and differing liturgical norms begin to bubble up in this conception of church, and the temptation to impose uniformity in place of unity creeps in. But a narrative ecclesiology demands that attention begin with particular histories, particular stories, particular depictions of the sacred, and particular practices, because in recognizing the uniqueness of each subject, we also recognize our shared humanity, our shared community, and through the *sensus fidei*, our shared faith. Stories are more effective than doctrines as building blocks of ecclesiology because they preserve subjectivity, allowing us to relate to an other in an act of empathic compenetration.[6] Moreover, the preservation

---

6. Goizueta, *Caminemos con Jesús*, 96: "Objects can only relate to one another externally . . . while subjects relate to each other through

of dangerous memories in historical narrative helps us resist the temptation to make Catholicism a homogenous community. "Homogenous communities impose unity by one of two means: exclusion or assimilation. Any other cultures will be either ostracized from the community . . . or they will be forced to surrender their particularity in order to participate in the community."[7] A worldwide church in a globalized society can be easily tempted by homogeneity, and uniformity can offer a facile substitute for unity, as all believers display the same beliefs and behaviors in lock step. But the existence of particular narratives resists this impulse. Scholars of the church should be engaged in retrieving and celebrating the cultural heterogeneity of the church in order to preserve as much particularity as possible. Only then can the people of God relate to one another as subjects and not objects, which is the basis of unity, a community of love.

The notion of connaturality, then, helps us understand the unity of the church as rooted in the particularity of narratives that draw us out of ourselves and also ring true within us. Understood as a function of connaturality, the unity of the church is based not on the suppression of cultural or liturgical particularity but on a deep appreciation for each genuine, particular tile in the mosaic of expressions of faith. Additionally, Goizueta's notion of particularity, especially as it reveals the universal, enables us to see the relationship between narrative and the universality, or catholicity, of the church. Building on José Vasconcelos's work on aesthetics in Latin American cultures, Goizueta notes that we can only appreciate true diversity in lived reality, not in logical abstractions. Goizueta uses the example of spousal love, where we can point to the difference between knowing about one's spouse and truly knowing him/her. Know-

---

empathic compenetration." I believe empathic compenetration is undoubtedly a component of connaturality.

7. Goizueta, *Caminemos con Jesús,* 98.

ing the facts of the other's existence or her features is not the same as being in relationship with an other. Logical rationality sees knowledge as the accumulation of facts, whereas aesthetic approaches delve into the particularity of an other, resulting in empathic unity.

> According to the quantitative, arithmetic criteria of logical rationality, in order to know the meaning of marriage we should marry as many persons as possible. Thus, the most knowledgeable person would be whoever has had the greatest number of particular spouses and has experienced the greatest number of particular marriages (perhaps a polygamist). According to the qualitative critera of the aesthetic sense, however, in order to know about "marriage," an abstract universal, one must enter fully into the depths of one particular marriage, engage one's life completely in the life of one other particular person, and, there—in that very particularity—uncover the universal meaning and significance of marriage.[8]

Universality is not founded on a gathering of as many individuals as possible but on delving deeply into the reality of a particular context. This is what reveals the universal. Analogously, the church cannot be known in its catholicity by merely adding up all the different liturgical variations and making them uniform, or by polling how many people believe a particular thing. Instead, the universality of the church is revealed in its particular manifestations, in the narratives of particular communities, in delving deeply and empathically into the story of an other. For this reason we must not hesitate to turn to art and storytelling when attempting to account for the universality of the church, because the universal exists not in opposition to the particular but as a result of it. Rather than a fragmented piece of pottery scattered throughout the

---

8. Ibid., 97.

world that must be pieced together into a whole, the universality of the church, like its unity, is more like a hologram, in which each piece reflects not part of a hologram but the whole. We should think of the church more in this hologram-style, which reflects the whole in each imperfect piece rather than imagining the universal global church as a single pot that is somehow shattered and scattered.

Storytelling and narrative help activate our sense of connaturality or unity with the other. In a compelling story, we see ourselves in the other, without reducing that experience to our own. We have all read books or seen art that draws us completely into another kind of culture or another kind of family relationship than the ones to which we are accustomed. We confront the reality of other lives regularly if we enter into relationships. One of the easiest ways to explain otherness and conscientization to undergraduates is to ask what life experience they thought was common to all people their age that when they came to college they discovered was actually something unique about their own families. When we come face to face with an other, be it another life, or culture, or way of making or eating dinner, we recognize the partial, peculiar nature of our own experience. This is the drawing-out aspect of connaturality: we are drawn to learn the experience of some other person's life because in doing this we understand our own in a different way. Thus, when scholars talk about a text or a piece of art resonating with a person, this resonance is not a reduction to sameness. Rather, it is like harmonization. A harmony requires at least two different sounds. Once we recognize that our customary experience is in fact subjective and partial, we understand human experience in a new way. But this requires entering into someone else's particularity, whether through art, relationship, proximity, or some other means. Neither does the partial nature of our experience necessarily mean that whatever experience is most common is the normative lens of all experience. In fact, the connaturality inherent in the *sensus fidei* also calls Christians to take up countercultural, prophetic stances at times.

The ITC names the *sensus fidei* as a supernatural instinct that "enables Christians to fulfill their prophetic calling."[9] The sense of the faithful exists not merely to assent to or confirm magisterial teaching or to recognize it when the gospel is presented in a top–down fashion. Instead, the supernatural instinct of faith, the connaturality that Christians have with the gospel that enables us to recognize it, also grounds the prophetic call of the people of God. A prophet exhorts people to draw near to God and bravely denounces those who would distance the people from God, even if they must denounce the powerful. In theologizing the laity through the lens of the *sensus fidei*, we must be open to the prophetic edge that lives in the disaffected, in the marginalized, and in the despised. At the same time, the ITC reminds us that we must not conflate people's ideas or understandings with the sense of the faithful. The sense of the faithful is an intuition, it is nondiscursive and therefore not reducible to ideas that, as the ITC document states, "circulate among the people of God." Here we must recall that people of God refers not only to the laity, however. The idea that not every instance of popular belief is compatible with faith has often been used to deride popular Catholic practices that originate in nondominant cultures like Latin American. But dominant cultures also circulate ideas that are incompatible with the faith. The *sensus fidei*, as the prophetic ground of the faithful, allows for critique and correction not only of one's own understanding of faith but of the understanding of those in power.

Features of a Third-Millennium Ecclesiology

The preceding chapters have examined different kinds of narratives, of varying genres, for their ecclesiological import.

---

9. ITC, "*Sensus Fidei* in the Life of the Church," 2.

Throughout, the stories of U.S. Latinos/as and their communities have featured prominently. U.S. Latinx history represents a dangerous memory that disrupts idealism about the United States as an uncomplicated context of successful immigrant Catholicism. Latina/o art and literature provide insight into the sense of the faithful, including the importance of everyday life in the story of the church. Literature, when approached as a theological source, also invites us to interpretation and dialogue, which is vital for any ecclesiology in the third millennium. By highlighting marginalized and subjugated voices, communities, and stories, narrative ecclesiology invites the church to make space for the other in its midst—in particular, for the despised other, and to give dialogue its proper place. In analyzing the demographic and ethnographic realities of different Latino/a communities, this ecclesiology demands attention to the difficult realities of deconversion and disaffiliation, as well as to the possibilities inherent in the church's long tradition of lay movements. So, while narrative ecclesiology might seem to focus more on narrative and less on ecclesial doctrine, what it in fact does is to connect these two realities through history, dialogue, and storytelling.

In order for ecclesiology to reorient itself, moving from a top–down, deductive process to a bottom–up, inductive discipline that begins with the reality of the people of God, it must undergo a methodological shift. Ecclesiologists can no longer proceed in a deductive fashion, where abstract principles about the nature and mission of the church are the starting point and the so-called practical applications are derived from these principles. An inductive approach begins with the reality of the people of God and draws its insights on the nature and mission of the church from that fertile ground. What sort of ecclesiology successfully weaves these narratives or makes use of them as source and resource moving into the third millennium of Christianity? Narrative ecclesiology must use historical narratives to preserve dangerous memory, literary narratives to surface the sense of the faithful and foster genuine dialogue, and demographic narratives to rekindle flexibility with respect to church structures.

Preserving Dangerous Memories

First, a narrative ecclesiology for the third millennium must preserve dangerous memories. Against the tendency to construct metanarratives that derive from abstract ecclesiological principles, the narrative ecclesiology proposed here embraces the Second Vatican Council's turn to human experience, the global nature of reality, and the ambiguity of history. Rather than deduce what it means for the church to be catholic from the plurality of meanings of the word "universality," for example, a narrative ecclesiology invites a telling of church history from the perspective of the marginalized, the despised, and the forgotten, and discovers the universality of the church in the particularity of those experiences. Delving into specific narratives of history, especially those that read "against the grain" of colonial or otherwise triumphalistic stories, reveals the universal character of God's saving action in history because this action happens in culturally, historically bound ways. What results resembles more of a mosaic of stories than a single, uniform grand narrative, along with the recognition that all stories are partial, as are all interpretations (hermeneutics). The partial character of human knowing necessitates relationship and dialogue, and this is a centerpiece of the church's unity and catholicity as well.

Methodologically, ecclesiologists could learn much from intercultural and intersectional methods that privilege human experience. María Pilar Aquino and Maricel Mena-López describe the method of intercultural dialogue as follows: "Intercultural perspectives require a dialectical intellectual praxis that allows social and cultural subjects to speak as equals and to forge alliances on the basis of their real conditions and their diverse contextualities for the purpose of achieving a common future of justice."[10] The process of intersectionality, then, must necessarily be collaborative, where genuine dialogue (which involves as much listening and interrogating of one's own position as it does speaking and articulating that position) reigns. By "intersectionality" I mean a move to recognize the complexity of embodied lives, the multiple communities and constituencies to which each of us belongs, and the ways in which different kinds of oppression are compounded upon one another for people marginalized by the dominant culture. This recognition prompts liberating action on a variety of fronts, so that we can no longer speak of, for example, the problem of sexism without also recognizing the intensifying effects that racism and classism have on women's lives.

Participants in intersectional methodologies view one another as co-creators of knowledge, not arbiters of truth. Admittedly, this step might prove difficult in a hierarchical church with a clerical, institutionalized magisterium. Nevertheless, ecclesiologists (who are increasingly laypeople) must attempt to engender this co-creative methodology. An essential part of this method for Aquino and Mena-López involves "relearning our thought by critically interpreting our own ways of living and thinking in our concrete contexts." They continue, "this relearning means entering into a process of suspecting our own suspicions and allowing our hermeneutics to be reorganized in relation to other hermeneutics."[11] Those who study the church must be prepared for their understandings of the nature and ministry of the church to be challenged by the story of the other. The human experience of church, especially in marginalized and silenced communities, deserves to be taken into ecclesiological account.

---

10. María Pilar Aquino and Maricel Mena-López, "Feminist Intercultural Theology: Religion, Culture, Feminism, and Power," in *Feminist Intercultural Theology* (Maryknoll: Orbis Books, 2007), xxxv.

11. Aquino and Mena-López, "Feminist Intercultural Theology," xxxvi.

Foregrounding the Sensus Fidei

Second, a narrative ecclesiology for the twenty-first century should foreground the *sensus fidei*, seeking it out wherever it is found. This book makes the case that a variety of aesthetic sources contain traces, and in some cases records and impressions, of the sense of the faithful. Art, literature, and the sacredness of everyday life (*lo cotidiano*) are vehicles for the *sensus fidei* to which ecclesiologists must attend. Stories are the cornerstone of human identity and therefore also of communal identity. Ecclesiologists can approach art and literature as a resource for theology when they see these artistic expressions depicting historical or cultural attitudes toward the church, personal and public devotions, and also (perhaps especially) when these aesthetic expressions record the dignity and sanctity of everyday life. Latinx theologians especially have noted that the sense of the faithful is embedded in popular religious practices, particularly popular Catholicism all over Latin America and the United States. But the intuition of the people of God is also revealed in the art, music, and literature produced by these communities.

In capturing beauty and truth, art of all kinds points to God's activity in the world. Popular Catholic practices such as a variety of Marian devotions might be depicted in literature or art, indicating to ecclesiologists where one aspect of the *sensus fidei* is operating. Moreover, many artistic expressions are described as sublime precisely because they elevate the ordinary to the realm of extraordinary beauty. This ordinary, everyday holiness attunes ecclesiologists to forgotten sectors of the church. After all, the church's holiness is not found merely in extraordinarily heroic acts of saintly perfection but in the frequent, unacknowledged acts of human kindness throughout *lo cotidiano*. This realm of the everyday, in part a private sphere that has been gendered feminine, is the arena of many women's saintly, overlooked perseverance. The ordinary, overlooked heroism of women's endurance in hardship, particularly Latinas, certainly constitutes a key part of the *sensus fidei* for Latinx theologians, writers, and artists.

Fostering Genuine Dialogue

Third, an ecclesiology for the third millennium must make room for the other and foster genuine dialogue among different constituencies in the church. It must be open to insights from unusual messengers, including secular literature. Allowing art to function not only as a data mine or resource but also as a source of theological insight refreshes ecclesiology in important ways. Our foray into the use of literature as source examined the symbiosis between the work of two Cuban women: Daína Chaviano and Ada María Isasi-Díaz. Chaviano's magical-realist novel, coupled with Isasi-Díaz's thoughts about the importance of place in our self-understanding, yielded a variety of important insights for those who wish to tell the church's story. Chaviano's text, set in the *periodo especial* in Cuba, resonates with the difficult ecclesial moment in the wake of the sexual-abuse and cover-up scandals and invites ecclesiologists to pay attention to the victims, to those outside the sightlines of the church's official story. Narrative ecclesiology should make room for more than the religious elites or virtuosi; it must dialogue with those struggling for survival on the margins, as Chaviano's protagonist is doing.

A further insight from the use of literature as a source is the importance for ecclesiology of maintaining identity-in-signification across times and cultures, which necessitates that narrative ecclesiologists privilege the principle of unity over uniformity. If our knowledge and hermeneutics are necessarily partial and not comprehensive, a certain amount of humility, even intellectual chastity, is required of ecclesiologists to recognize that new stories are always emerging and new ecclesiological syntheses are possible, even desirable, as the church lives into the global reality most succinctly theo-

rized by Karl Rahner in 1968.[12] Thus, an overarching uniformity does not necessarily convey the gospel, and may distort
it, in a variety of cultures of the global church. Rahner notes
immediately after Vatican II that "Theology, however, will
go on living, renewing continually its strength and vitality.
Corresponding to the Council itself, it will become a world-
theology: that is it will exist in the non-European, non-North
American countries, but no longer merely as an export from
the West."[13] Exporting ecclesiology from the church's center
to its margins fails to take into account the reality that the
church is a multicultural, multilocal, global reality, and that
cultures express the reality of salvation in ways intelligible
to their own contexts. A narrative ecclesiology, as a mosaic
or tapestry of stories, becomes a world ecclesiology through
dialogue, through making room for the other, giving not
only space but *proper* place to the voices of the victimized
and the silenced.

A final insight from examining literature as a source for
theology is the multi-sites reality of the church. Drawing on
the work of Isasi-Díaz in conjunction with Chaviano's novel,
we see the importance of mapping the multi-site nature of
the church—that the church emerges and continues to exist
not only from the center outward, but that there is a dyna-
mism from the margins in all directions, not merely toward
the center. This sense of displacement and multiple belonging crystallizes in Chaviano's protagonist and in Isasi-Díaz's
life (as well as the lives of Latinas everywhere, who belong
to several cultures at once and no culture exclusively). These
women are a crucial metaphor for global Catholicism, which
seeks a church that is alive in many places but never fully at
home, never complacent with the status quo; a church that

---

12. Karl Rahner, "The Abiding Significance of the Second Vatican
Council," in *Concern for the Church,* Theological Investigations 20 (New
York: Crossroad, 1981), 90–102.

13. Rahner, "Abiding Significance," 95–96.

is in a state of eschatological in-between-ness between the already and the not-yet of God's reign—a church that is multilocal and displaced and searching for meaning from this middle place of flux. Analyzing the complexity of the present moment reveals the complexity of the past history (of the church or any social, political, or religious entity), and mitigates against nostalgia and idealism. Narrative ecclesiology must map the multi-site reality that is the church and use this map to proclaim the kerygma in ways that are culturally intelligible and doctrinally coherent.

Engendering Flexibility in Church Structures

Fourth, and finally, a narrative ecclesiology for the twenty-first century must engender flexibility in church structures. Demographic and sociological data make clear that lay initiatives are supplanting parishes as the primary place of ecclesial encounter. Are we prepared to tell the stories of these lay initiatives, or to let the groups contribute their stories to the church's? Pew, CARA, and many other sources have clearly documented a rise in unaffiliated persons, "nones," as well as a desire for what Kaya Oakes has termed DIY religion, or self-made spirituality. Part of hearing wisdom from unusual and unexpected sources should be from these unaffiliated, or differently affiliated persons in our midst. Because such a large number of "former Catholics" now identify themselves as having no particular church, ecclesiologists are called to examine (1) what constitutes membership in the church, (2) what the sense of the faithful is regarding church affiliation, and (3) how the message of the gospel is and can be communicated most effectively. Part of this task is examining the tradition for alternatives to the territorial-parish model that has reigned in the United States since the middle of the last century.

A historical look at the Iberian Catholicism that was imported to the Americas in the sixteenth century reveals different emphases from the ones that dominate Northern

European Catholicism. As it has evolved and inculturated throughout Latin America and the South and Southwest United States, Latinx Catholicism instantiates many of the characteristics of the pre-Tridentine Iberian faith the colonizers brought to these shores. Among the trends that continue in present practice are an emphasis on local devotion, on bonds of family and friendship, shared affinity for a saint or a spiritual practice over geographic ties, and a proliferation of extraparochial groups, many of them led by the laity.

Though by no means homogenous across the many cultures and cultural admixtures of Latin America (since there is no such thing as a "pure culture"), the Latin American peoples who found themselves in the United States through a variety of different circumstances of migration share a rootedness in a different sort of Catholic belonging and practice. As a result, these cultural groups, frequently marginalized in territorial parishes in the United States, are uniquely prepared to usher in a new paradigm. Rather than view U.S. Latinx populations as anomalous when it comes to resisting disaffiliation (a claim unsupported by data that shows Latinos/as moving away from Catholicism toward Pentecostalism or no church), perhaps ecclesiology could look at aspects of Latinx religiosity as a strategy for resilience in times of great flux. The DIY religion of the nones, who forge their own paths of spirituality in the absence of clergy or a welcoming community, has much in common with the popular Catholicism of rural Latin Americans who had little regular access to clergy but nonetheless persisted in prayer and mutual support. Lay-led initiatives seem a demographic inevitability given the graying clergy population and the decades-long decline in vocations to the all-male celibate priesthood. When the institutional church fails to offer welcome and support for people who are struggling with migration, Latinx Catholics found a way to continue to supplement their institutional Catholicism with home-based practices, family customs, prayer groups, faith-based social activism, public processions, and other devotions. Indeed, some theorists would flip this paradigm, insisting that popular Catholicism is in fact the people's primary expression of faith, and the institutional piece is a supplement to those expressions of faith. In either case, it is clear that Latinx Catholics, accustomed to a shortage of clergy, have been operating in the current U.S. demographic reality of clergy shortfall for some time, especially throughout rural areas of Latin America. Lay empowerment and popular religion thrived then and could continue to be the answer now.

But engendering flexibility in church structures does not mean that the laity should be flexible about accepting changes imposed from a top–down mentality, or tolerating the closing of more parishes and the consolidation of power into fewer and fewer hands. Instead, flexibility should mean more openness to new and emerging paradigms of governance, of leadership, and of spirituality. Not unlike the mid-sixteenth century, when the church in the throes of the crisis of the Reformation was willing to revisit ancient paradigms for church organization, so too in the present moment of disaffiliation and crisis of moral authority should the institutional church be willing to open itself to emerging paradigms of lay leadership and lay initiative. Flexibility and nimbleness are not unidirectional, where the clergy demand flexibility and the laity must display it. On the contrary, the very words evoke a multidimensional willingness to step outside old, brittle structures into new life: new wine, new wineskins.

Some might object that disaffiliation should not be a major concern to theologians because the church is not a business trying to attract customers or a team aiming to keep loyal fans. This is quite true. The church's mission is to preach the gospel throughout the world, and frequently this evangelization is countercultural, that is, it countervails contemporary cultural trends. Why, then, should the church attend to the sense of the faithful, or popular religious practices, or the opinions of those who have declared themselves no longer Catholic? How should the church balance its desire to combat the trend of disaffiliation and demographic change with its obligation to preach the gospel regardless of its popularity?

I find the answer lies in three key insights. First, the church cannot be accused of chasing fads or being trendy when it discerns the signs of the times and interprets these in light of the gospel, as *Gaudium et Spes* suggests. This discernment and interpretation are fundamental to the church's mission in the world. The preaching of the good news depends on the gospel being heard; it depends on intelligibility.

This is the second insight. We learn from the scene at Pentecost, when the multitude heard the gospel in intelligible ways, that the act of evangelization requires a preacher and a hearer. If part of the task of ecclesiology (and indeed of all theology) is to maintain identity-in-signification when it comes to the gospel, then as language and cultural paradigms shift, the church, both *ad extra* and *ad intra,* must reexamine whether the gospel message is rendered unintelligible in the way it is being preached. If the territorial parishes are empty, devoid of life and enthusiasm, if there are no hearers there, can there be evangelization there? Put another way, is the fundamental mission of the church frustrated by ossifying structures? Ecclesiology cannot allow the church's mission to be hindered by its cultural circumstances, because the gospel transcends cultural circumstances even though, as linguistic, it is always already culturally bound.

Third and most important, we should not dismiss as trend chasing the act of discerning where people's energy is found, because frequently in the church's history this is where the Holy Spirit is found. The *sensus fidelium* is astir in lay-led movements, in social-justice movements, in groups that foster lay empowerment in a variety of arenas in the church. Searching the tradition for alternative ecclesial paradigms reveals that many communities living in the United States are already taking part in these alternative visions of church. The church changes in this way: not because a group of bishops declares that a new paradigm will now be enforced, but because the people of God live into a new paradigm, a new vision, at times in fits and starts until this paradigm makes the most sense for the most people. We would not arrive at the sixteenth-century surge in monasticism and new religious orders by way of a focus group. Any ecclesiologist who looks at that period sees the work of the Holy Spirit.

So, too, we must search for the movement of the Spirit in the lives of present-day Catholics. Pneumatology, as expressed in the *sensus fidelium*, cannot be retroactive. The Spirit continues to work in the people of God today. Are we willing to listen to the wisdom of the Spirit, even if it comes to us from nontraditional sources like the disaffiliated or disaffected?

Looking Ahead

Incorporating narrative into ecclesiology, indeed reorienting ecclesiology so that it is narrative based, ensures that we look to the future realistically but also optimistically.

Realistically, the future of the church looks somewhat bleak, given the disaffiliation trends tracked by scholars. The Latino/a community (both immigrant and U.S.-born), though frequently cited as the future of the Catholic Church, is nevertheless also showing trends that move away from Roman Catholicism and toward Pentecostalism and religious disaffiliation. The sociopolitical environment of the United States is polarized and in many ways toxic to dialogue and interculturality. The ecclesial environment must do more than resist this reality; it must actively work toward embracing those who are silenced and on the margins. In the church's long history, new forms of association have welled up in religious orders, monastic communities, and lay associations. Times of upheaval have the potential to yield great fruitfulness if we are courageous and humble enough to listen to the rumblings of the Holy Spirit. If ecclesiologists are willing to undertake a radical reimagining of the church, what might it look like? Is the fundamental mission of the church about access to the sacramental ministry? Is it about fellowship in communion with one another? Is the church fundamentally about social transformation? How can each of these three elements of the church's mission be facilitated most effectively? By listening to the stories of Catholics—those who remain in the church and those who have left disillusioned—we can envision a way forward through the bleak present.

The future looks anti-institutional. The moral and ethical failures of the institutional church are no longer secrets discussed in closed rooms. In reality, the church has been revealed to be vulnerable to the temptations of insularity, self-protection, and other forms of corruption. These grave faults, and the scandals of mismanagement that have accompanied the church in the last two decades, have caused or reinforced some of the anti-institutional sentiment that was brewing among younger Catholics.

But the church is more than its failings, and, to use one example, Pope Francis's recent emphases on the joy of the gospel and the need for mercy help rebuild institutional credibility. Attempts at foregrounding justice issues and contextualizing the sexual ethics that dominated the church's public face for so long are helpful, but the anti-institutional tide is broader even than an institution as formidable as the Catholic Church. Rather than trying to steer millennials and future generations toward trusting in institutions, ecclesiologists might rethink the ways in which the church's mission is to listen and learn from the signs of the times. Interfaith partnerships, intergenerational communities, and other forms of collaborative work engage young people in meaningful dialogue and work for justice. A more participatory view of the church's mission shows promise in an environment that distrusts institutions.

Lastly, the future looks more diffuse but no less intense

when it comes to spiritual seeking. A decline in emphasis on geographic proximity that gives way to a rise in emphasis on bonds of affinity might help the church navigate the next few decades of dominance by the "nones." This affinity need not be merely political, and, in fact, bonds of political affinity tend to be brittle. Instead, affinity based in spiritual or social praxis, in alliances on behalf of the common good, point the way forward in this diffuse context. Many of these affinity groups already exist and have historically existed—not just in the U.S. church, and not just all over Latin America, but over the rest of the world. Like the generations before them, these Christians too have a story that needs to be told.

Index

academic theologians, as *hembra*, 76, 77, 78
Academy of Catholic Hispanic Theologians of the United States (ACHTUS), x, 11, 15
ACU. *See* Agrupación Católica Universitaria
aesthetics, and *sensus fidei*, 149
Agrupación Católica Universitaria, 100, 120–28
  in contemporary United States, 124, 125, 128–29
  impact of, 130–32
  material and professional success of members, 130, 131
  and service to local church, 127, 128
American Catholicism, multilocal origins, 9
Anzaldúa, Gloria, on the image of Guadalupe, 53
Aquino, María Pilar
  on intercultural character of Latino/a theology, 17, 18, 22
  on intercultural dialogue, 147, 148
  on *lo cotidiano*, 25
Argüedas, José María, 34
art
  as source and resource for ecclesiology/theology, 32,

33, 36, 37, 50–56, 59–63, 87, 137, 138, 140–46, 149, 150
  visual, as text, 50
  women's, and holiness, 57–61
  women's, and *sensus fidelium*, 62

Badillo, David, on Iberian origins of Latin American Catholicism, 112, 113
Balseros, 67
Balthasar, Hans Urs von, 35, 61
Batista, Fulgencio, 122
"The Battle of the Virgins" (Rosario Ferré), 36, 37–50

Carr, Anne, on the people of God, 4
Carroll, Coleman, 124, 126
Castro, Fidel, 122, 123, 125, 127
Catholic Church
  during Castro regime in Cuba, 123
  disaffiliation from, 66, 79, 97, 100, 101, 104, 105, 156
  período especial of, 79
  threats to, as social force, 70
Catholicism, nonimmigrant Latinx, 8, 9
Center for Applied Research in the Apostolate (CARA), on U.S. religious landscape, 97, 97n1, 152